MY HOUR

1 3 5 7 9 10 8 6 4 2

Yellow Jersey Press
20 Vauxhall Bridge Road,
London SW1V 2SA

Yellow Jersey Press is part of the Penguin Random House group of companies
whose addresses can be found at global.penguinrandomhouse.com

First published by Yellow Jersey in 2015

www.vintage-books.co.uk

A CIP catalogue record for this book is available from the British Library

ISBN 9780224100465

Printed and bound in Italy by L.E.G.O. Spa

Penguin Random House is committed to a sustainable future for our business,
our readers and our planet. This book is made from Forest Stewardship
Council® certified paper

BRADLEY WIGGINS
MY HOUR

with William Fotheringham

HIGH LIFE HIGHLAND	
3800 15 0042853 1	
Askews & Holts	Jan-2016
B WIG	£20.00

Yellow Jersey Press

For Cath, Ben and Bella

0 minutes

INTRODUCTION BY
CHRIS BOARDMAN

Even though I've known him for more than a decade, Sir Bradley Wiggins still remains something of an enigma to me, which is why I find him fascinating.

He's an incredible athlete and in many ways unique. After everything he's done, including winning the Tour de France, the greatest race in the world, with all the ambition and passion that must have taken, he's comfortable with coming to a race like the Tour of Britain – as he did at the end of 2015 – and riding around being a team rider like anyone else. He is a bundle of contradictions. I remember attending the BBC Sports Personality of the Year, when Brad was nominated. Each athlete walked on to the brightly lit stage to do their bit with Sue Barker, where they thanked their teams, sponsors, families and coaches, a totally understandable but undeniably bland thing to watch. Then Brad steps on to the platform and everyone holds their breath. Is he going to swear, put two fingers up, or give the most eloquent speech you can possibly imagine? Bland Brad is not. Some might find his volatility unsettling – some sponsors probably do – but one thing Brad isn't is boring and, in this PC day and age, that is something worth watching, the kind of character I think we need in the world of sport: someone who offers more than athletic prowess and politeness, someone who shows character.

It was after a phone call in January 2003 from the then Great Britain Performance Director Peter Keen – who had been my coach when I was riding – that I began working with Brad and his then coach Simon Jones. 'We've got this lad who is very good, podium standard in fact, but he's frustrated by finishing second and has decided he wants to ditch working with the GB squad and go to ride for a French pro team full time. Listening to him, it all seems really woolly and he's so close to making a breakthrough, I'm worried he's going to throw it all away. You've done all the things he is trying to achieve so he'll listen to you; would you mind having a word with him?'

Our first conversation at the velodrome in Manchester later that month confirmed Pete's concerns: the passion was there but the plans to achieve his stated goals just didn't add up. It sounded very much like someone reverse engineering a rationale to justify the actions they wanted to take . . . and it wasn't very convincing. But it wasn't me who had to be convinced.

I think the biggest advantage I had over Brad's advisers at the time (who were all smarter than me) is that I wasn't really bothered if he succeeded. I had no direct interest in the outcome, which might sound callous, but often to fix something you have to be

prepared to break it. Who better to take that risk than someone who is expendable? I could afford to be honest to the point of being offensive, and the worst that could happen was that they wouldn't want to speak to me again.

Sitting at a table in the Manchester Velodrome canteen, I asked Brad to outline his ideas for me. To his credit and to my surprise, he was brave enough to put up with my blunt and dogged probing of his plans, such as they were. Why are you going to France? How is riding that stage race there going to help your preparation for the pursuit? Is that enough time to recover? Where is your rest period? The conversation was followed by a written plan and – I'm embarrassed to say now – I went through it with a red pen in the most patronising way. Again to my surprise, he stuck with it, willing to subject himself to harsh criticism and examine his own ideas. Realising that many of them were pretty flimsy when put under the spotlight, it was less than a week before he came to the conclusion that his proposed actions were not likely to bring him the success he was after. He would stay with his coach Simon Jones and together they'd tackle the 2003 season. And that was it: they were off. By the end of the year he had become pursuit champion of the world and 12 months later an Olympic gold medallist.

Over that amazing period, my role with the pair was minimal; they gave me a mandate to act as sounding board and hold up the mirror. I was someone they knew they could get honest feedback from, someone who had done the things that they were setting out to achieve, and someone who clearly had nothing riding on the result.

Even after he became Olympic pursuit champion, I certainly wouldn't have predicted that Brad would end up winning the Tour de France. I doubt he would have either. Even as late as 2010, when Dave Brailsford started Team Sky with the stated goal of winning the Tour in five years with a British rider, I'm not ashamed to admit that I raised my eyebrows along with everyone else.

Coming from the track to win the Tour was something that simply didn't happen in modern cycling. But together, Dave, Brad and their team approached the tasks as they had every sporting challenge so far: one step at a time. As soon as a goal was achieved, they reached for the next one, like climbing a mountain, focusing not on the summit, just on the next few steps. Brad went from winning prologue time trials, to stages, to becoming a stage-race overall contender. Each success had its own reward, for sure, but each led immediately to the next, even more stretching challenge, until amazingly, in that incredible summer of 2012, they found themselves challenging for the top step of the most important podium in the world for a cyclist: the Tour de France.

I didn't work with Brad for those last few years; once he had become Olympic champion he had all the confidence and self-belief he needed, so my part was done; but he kept working with smart people, was always part of a cutting-edge team of coaches, managers and mentors, people who came to realise that if they put the work in, this man

would deliver. And that ability to perform under pressure attracted some of the very best: Simon Jones, Matt Parker and, most recently, Tim Kerrison.

In many ways, the Hour was the perfect project for Brad: it tapped into a career's-worth of learning, everything he was good at could be utilised in this most specialised of challenges. In late January 2015, I made a brief visit to a Team Sky training camp in Majorca and we sat down for an hour to talk about his plans for the event I was probably more familiar with than anyone else in the world. Again, I just asked questions about the project but, unlike the gangly youth I'd known in 2003, this time he had all the elements in place. In fact, everything he'd been doing for the last decade was about to come into play: pursuiting had taught him pace judgement and technical skill, hours in the wind tunnel had honed his position, and dealing with the pressure in the Tour de France would allow him to cope with the unique stresses of this event. The only element beyond his control was the weather . . .

Perhaps unavoidably for a high-profile sportsperson, Brad was obliged to commit to a date rather than look for a window of opportunity for his attempt, and, as it turned out, luck was not on his side. His scheduled start time coincided with one of the highest air pressure days London had experienced that year and, as 90 per cent of the energy expended by a rider is used up pushing the air out of the way, that fact cost him close to a kilometre. Many would have looked for another opportunity to maximise their distance but, true to form, for Brad that was it – one shot and he'd moved on, leaving the fans to wonder just what he could have achieved in ideal conditions.

People think an Hour Record is just a matter of riding around in circles until you are told to stop, but, although it may look like a closed-road time trial, many have found to their cost that it's not. Against the clock on the road, you have the opportunity for 'micro rests', fractions of a second when changing gear, or getting out of the saddle when possible to ease off the pressure for a moment. Similarly in a time trial if you overextend and push your body into the red, descents and corners offer an opportunity to recover, to reset. In the Hour, you carry any mistakes with you until the end, so pacing is everything for this the most deceivingly delicate of events.

I've always thought of pacing as an equation consisting of three questions: how far –or how long – is there still to go? How hard am I trying? Is this sustainable? In the Hour, if the answer to the last one is 'yes', then you aren't going hard enough. If it's 'no', it's already too late. The unnerving answer you're looking for is 'maybe'. To complicate matters, why the event isn't about measuring pulse or power and riding to a number is that the effort to elicit that ambiguous answer is constantly changing depending on where you are; with three minutes to go it's a wholly different effort compared to having 40 minutes left to race.

The Hour is for aficionados, for the people who love cycling history. Outside the sport, you have to explain it. For the last of my own three attempts – the Athlete's Hour as it became known – on a standard round-tubed bike, I wanted it to be something people could believe in at face value, I wanted the UCI (Union Cycliste Internationale) to take urine samples and freeze them (which they refused to do at the time, something I bet they regret now) so people could watch and have faith that what they were seeing was an athlete and that was it.

It is at once a complex and wonderfully simple challenge. Spectators empathise with what the athlete is going through and appreciate the risk they take; in the Hour you don't do 'a good ride': you either succeed or you fail with the world watching.

If Brad does not reschedule a second attempt to get better climatic conditions then it shouldn't surprise anyone; he has always ploughed his own furrow. Most athletes win the Tour de France then go on to have a career in the Grand Tours. For him, once was enough. He'd got the thing he wanted and then couldn't sustain the passion to put himself through it all again. And so he took cycling's most prestigious record and will probably never attempt it again. He is certainly a great in terms of results and, although many will try to find him a pigeonhole, to compare him with champions past, I really don't think we should. He's a one-off.

It's been fascinating watching him both close up and from a distance. Sometimes he makes us cringe, sometimes he disappoints, other times he produces breathtaking performances and makes eloquent speeches. He is unpredictable but, above all, he is authentic, something we see less and less in the increasingly commercialised world of sport. As he heads towards the close of his career, people will still flock to see him because of that: maybe he'll launch an audacious attack . . . or maybe Sir Brad will languish in the bunch for the duration. You just never know, and I think that's wonderful.

7 minutes

ALL THE SEVENS –
PLATFORMS OF HOPE

Numbers ending in 7 stick in my head, so when I went through the longest 60 minutes of my life in the London Olympic velodrome, these were the points on the clock that ended up as staging posts along the way: 7 minutes, 17, 27... up to the moment of relief where I had been riding for 57 minutes and I knew the pain was about to end.

Previous page: *The Lee Valley VeloPark. The Olympic stadium was built on the site of the old Eastway Cycle Circuit that I used to ride on when I was in my teens*

Numbers help me get through any event I'm competing in: an Olympic pursuit, a time trial or a mountain stage in the Tour de France. Platforms of hope, that's what I call them. They are part of the mental game I use to push myself on. I never think, 'God, this is hard, I can't do it any more.' Instead, I cast my mind ahead and try to imagine how I'll feel when I'm a little bit further on. I've always done this. It helps to keep my spirits up. In 2012, when I was climbing through the Alps and the Pyrenees on my way to winning the Tour, on those massive mountain passes I would be thinking, 'Two kilometres from now you're only going to have one kilometre left and how are you going to feel then? You'll have done it'. It was the same in the Olympic time trial at Hampton Court: 'Five kilometres from now you'll have another five to go, and you can do that easily'. It's almost like cutting a corner in your head.

Finding those staging posts matters as much in the Hour Record as it does in the Tour de France; those 60 minutes are much more demanding mentally than physically. Of course, riding as far as I could in an hour was hard on my body given the conditions and so on, but it was no tougher than riding up Mont Ventoux in 2009 knowing that fourth place overall in my breakthrough Tour de France was on the line, or finishing empty in a long time trial, like I did at Chartres when I won the 2012 Tour. What blows your mind as you ride the Hour is watching the time tick away, minute after minute, looking

Spectators start to arrive. The
venue sold out its 6,000 capacity
in just 7 minutes following tickets
going on sale

at the computer screen held by up your coach every 16 seconds. Every one of those 218 laps.

You can't escape that countdown. It takes over everything for that Hour. And that is what made it a harder challenge mentally. That, put together with the fact that I had known for the previous six months that I was going for the Hour on 7 June 2015 in front of a sell-out crowd of 6,000 in the London Olympic velodrome, live on TV with over a million people watching, with absolutely nowhere to hide. It would be just me in that velodrome, with no one else on the track to draw the attention away if I put a foot wrong. You play all that down beforehand – oh yeah, I'm going to thrive off it on the day. When it's done you look back and think, 'God, I was under a lot of pressure there.' That's why you need every mind game you can come up with.

The organisers had asked me what music I wanted them to put on the PA as I entered the track centre, and what I wanted to hear while I waited for the starter's gun. I asked for the Prodigy's 'Firestarter' for when I was in the gate – from my youth, quite pumped up, a bit punky. For my entrance into the velodrome I asked for 'Stone Love' by the Supremes, purely because when the Stone Roses did their comeback tour in 2012 they always used to come onstage to that. I don't actually know if they played them or not, because the noise was so deafening on the day: the crowd drowned it all out. It was bizarre coming up into the track and finding a full house. For seven weeks I'd been training in empty velodromes around Europe, and now this.

So here I am, sitting on the start line, desperate to get on with it, wanting to get going. I'm not really aware what time it is – I know the attempt is meant to be at 6.30 p.m. It feels as if I finished my warm-up long ago – the usual British Cycling warm-up, 15 to 20 minutes – and I've got that sense that if I wait any longer now I'll need to do it all over again. I've done my couple of laps of the track, the bike's already in the gate: let's do this, let's go, I want to get on with this. It's only afterwards I learn that I got out of the start gate during an ad break, so live television missed the moment.

This has been on my mind since January. The date has been set in stone since then. There has been so much expectation, so much hype, but it has been a lonely existence for the last 24 hours. It's dawned on me already and I'm thinking it now: no one can help any more. There is no one else to rely on, no one to do it for me. It's just me and the clock. All the training has been done and now everyone has come to watch me. It feels a bit like going to the gallows. I want to get on with it. I don't want to sit here any longer. I don't want to go through another few minutes thinking about it. I'm just ready to go.

It took seven weeks to get to that start line in London – I rode my last race for Team Sky, Paris–Roubaix, on 12 April – but my personal history with the Hour goes back a lot further than that. Throughout my teens and just beyond there was a spate of attempts as one star after another took up the challenge. It began at Easter in 1993 when I was nearly 13 and watched Graeme Obree going for the British record at Herne Hill, and after that there were at least half a dozen attempts by the likes of Chris Boardman, Miguel Indurain and Tony Rominger, so I soon got to know what the record was all about.

Like all British cyclists, I was blown away when Graeme smashed Francesco Moser's Hour in Norway in July 1993. And a few weeks later Boardman was on my television screen after he'd broken the record in Bordeaux. He'd done it on the day the Tour came to town and so was standing on the podium alongside Indurain, who was wearing the yellow jersey that day. That week my copy of *Cycling Weekly* came with a free poster of Chris on the Bordeaux velodrome going for the record in his North Wirral Velo-Kodak kit.

The year after that, Indurain broke the record after the Tour, then Tony Rominger, then Chris again with his 56.375km in 1996. But after that the UCI put their oar in. They had seen one development after another in aerodynamics – mainly from Graeme with his radical positions, the bent-arm tuck and the stretched-arm 'Superman' – and felt too much attention was being paid to the bikes rather than the cyclists. So in 1997 they tried to turn the clock back by putting all the Hour Records that had been done using aero kit since the 1970s into a category of their own, called Best Human Performance, while the way they wanted the Hour to be done – and the record they wanted to promote – would have riders using kit similar to the stuff Eddy Merckx had used in 1972: drop handlebars rather than tri-bars or Graeme's tuck position; old-school spoked wheels, leather 'hairnet' crash-hat not tear-drop aero-hat, and so on.

Arriving at the track ahead of the attempt with my soigneur *Pete Smith. I went for a shave and haircut in the morning. The hairdresser asked if I was doing anything interesting today. 'Not really,' I said*

The UCI named this the Athlete's Hour; the last Hour I watched was the first of these, Chris's Athlete's Hour at the world track championships in Manchester in 2000. I was 20 years old, the GB team had won a bronze in the team pursuit at the Olympics in Sydney earlier that summer, and we were riding the team pursuit at the Worlds that week. I sat in the track centre next to Graeme Obree and watched Chris going through his 60 minutes. The Athlete's Hour looked incredibly hard; it seemed like it would be really painful staying in that position, and when I asked Chris about it later he said he couldn't walk for days. It didn't look like something you'd want to try.

So why did I want to have a go myself 15 years later? For one thing, I knew the history. I'd witnessed bits of it for myself, but there was more to the Hour than the rides plastered across my teens. The record dates back to 1893; the first official holder was a Frenchman, Henri Desgrange, who then went on to found the Tour de France ten years after that. The Hour taps into the most basic questions for any cyclist: how far can you go and how fast? Until the UCI changed the rules, the Hour was a record that was truly of its time: it was held by the guy who was the fastest under whatever the conditions were at a given moment in cycling history. There was a long gap through the 1970s and early 1980s when no one dared go for Merckx's record – but that just reflected the way Eddy was seen at the time. Eddy had described riding the Hour as the hardest thing he'd done in

'It's such a simple idea, but it's brutal as well: you are on your own in the velodrome, with nowhere to hide. There are no prizes for effort or silver medals for coming second. You either beat the record . . . or you fail, and you do so in front of as many people as you choose to have watching. And they are watching one person: you.'

his career. If that was what the greatest cyclist in the sport's history felt, you can see why people were afraid of having a go. Everyone had seen the pictures of Eddy being lifted off his bike afterwards because he couldn't stand, and it was a scary prospect.

Chris's 56.375km in 1996 has now taken on the same stature: he did it using Obree's Superman position, which was super-fast, Chris was on outstanding form and the conditions were ideal, almost freakish. That means many people feel it will never be beaten. But the scariness and the suffering that the Hour brings are part of the attraction, and it's why it has never really gone out of date. It's such a simple idea, but it's brutal as well: you are on your own in the velodrome, with nowhere to hide. There are no prizes for effort or silver medals for coming second. You either beat the record, even if it's by a single metre, or you fail, and you do so in front of as many people as you choose to have watching. And they are watching one person: you.

And then there's the romance it has acquired over the years. To start with, there are the names of the holders: Fausto Coppi, Roger Rivière, Ole Ritter, Eddy Merckx, Jacques Anquetil. They all have something about them: Coppi and Rivière, the tragic heroes, who died too young; Ritter, the complete obsessive; Merckx, the greatest ever; and 'Master Jacques', the ultimate cycling machine. Then there are the background stories: Coppi set his record in Milan in 1942 in between bombing raids by the RAF, and then pretty much

'I felt that if I was doing the Hour Record then it should be about pleasing the public as well as about the physical performance – it would be open house with everyone invited, it would be a big event and it would be televised. I didn't ever consider doing it any other way.'

1893
HENRI DESGRANGE
French
35.325 km

1972
EDDY MERCKX
Belgian
49.431 km

1984
FRANCESCO MOSER
Italian
51.151 km

THE HOUR RECORD (in km)

1893 HENRI DESGRANGE Paris **35.325**

1894 JULES DUBOIS Paris **38.220**

1897 OSCAR VANDEN EYNDE Paris **39.240**

1898 WILLIE HAMILTON Denver **40.781**

1905 LUCIEN PETIT-BRETON Paris **41.110**

1907 MARCEL BERTHET Paris **41.520**

1912 OSCAR EGG Paris **42.360**

1913 MARCEL BERTHET Paris **42.741**

1913 OSCAR EGG Paris **43.525**

1913 MARCEL BERTHET Paris **43.775**

1914 OSCAR EGG Paris **44.247**

1933 JAN VAN HOUT Holland **44.588**

1933 MAURICE RICHARD Belgium **44.777**

1935 GIUSEPPE OLMO Milan **45.090**

1936 MAURICE RICHARD Milan **45.325**

1937 FRANS SLAATS Milan **45.485**

1937 MAURICE ARCHAMBAUD Milan **45.767**

1942 FAUSTO COPPI Milan **45.798**

1956 JACQUES ANQUETIL Milan **46.159**

1956 ERCOLE BALDINI Milan **46.394**

■ THE ATHLETE'S HOUR   ■ THE UNIFIED HOUR RECORD

1994
GRAEME OBREE
British
52.713 km

1996
CHRIS BOARDMAN
British
56.375 km

2015
BRADLEY WIGGINS
British
54.526 km

1957 ROGER RIVIÈRE Milan **46.923**

1959 ROGER RIVIÈRE Milan **47.347**

1967 FERDI BRACKE Rome **48.093**

1968 OLE RITTER Mexico City **48.653**

1972 EDDY MERCKX Mexico City **49.431**

1984 FRANCESCO MOSER Mexico City **50.808**

1984 FRANCESCO MOSER Mexico City **51.151**

1993 GRAEME OBREE Norway **51.596**

1993 CHRIS BOARDMAN Bordeaux **52.270**

1994 GRAEME OBREE Bordeaux **52.713**

1994 MIGUEL INDURAIN Bordeaux **53.040**

1994 TONY ROMINGER Bordeaux **53.832**

1994 TONY ROMINGER Bordeaux **55.291**

1996 CHRIS BOARDMAN Manchester **56.375**

2000 CHRIS BOARDMAN Manchester **49.441**

2005 ONDŘEJ SOSENKA Moscow **49.700**

2014 JENS VOIGT Grenchen, Switzerland **51.110**

2014 MATTHIAS BRÄNDLE Aigle, Switzerland **51.852**

2015 OHAN DENNIS Grenchen, Switzerland **52.491**

2015 ALEX DOWSETT Manchester **52.937**

2015 BRADLEY WIGGINS London **54.526**

The rule change in late 2014 by
the UCI allowing for bikes with a
standard time-trial set-up was one
of the major reasons why I felt I
could take on the record

marched off to fight for Italy in the war, was taken prisoner in North Africa and spent a year as a prisoner of war. Anquetil's reputation began when he broke Coppi's record with his first attempt – he made another at the end of his career but it was disallowed as he refused a drugs test. And then there was Merckx going for it just the once, in his prime, travelling to Mexico to ride at altitude, and then having to be carried away afterwards. Later on, Francesco Moser brought cycling into the aerodynamic era in 1984 by using a whole raft of innovative kit. Finally, there was the fantastic battle between Obree and Boardman in the mid-1990s, when they would fight it out in the national 25-mile time trial championship alongside club riders from around the country, then pop off somewhere seemingly exotic like Norway or Bordeaux to put their names in the record books alongside those greats.

I started thinking about the Hour when the UCI changed the rules in May 2014 after Brian Cookson took over as president. The new rule allowed a bike with a current time-trial set-up to be used. There were no limiting factors. To be honest the record was a relatively easy target at that point because it had been reset back to a mark set by Ondrej Sosenka, a little-known Czech who rode 49.700km in 2005, which wasn't much further than Merckx had gone in 1972; and on a current bike with twenty-first-century aerodynamic kit you'd expect to get over 50km relatively comfortably. I don't think Chris Boardman's 1996 distance of 56.375km is out of reach on the right day in Manchester, but it's a far more daunting target than any of the distances set immediately after the UCI relaunched the record. I would never have considered attempting the Hour if the UCI hadn't changed the rules. None of us would have done.

Jens Voigt was the first rider to try the Hour after the rule change. He beat Francesco Moser's record of 51.151km – although he didn't get past Graeme Obree's distance from 1993 – and that gave confidence to all of us who had an interest in having a go as well. There was a spate of attempts after Jens went for it: Matthias Brändle in October 2014, Jack Bobridge in January 2015, Rohan Dennis, Sarah Storey and Gustav Larsson in February, Thomas Dekker in March and Alex Dowsett in May of the same year. It was a case of everyone rushing to get their name on the board. But Jens's attempt in September 2014 was where that run started, so the sport has a lot to thank him for.

I couldn't help thinking, 'I'd expect to have three minutes on Jens on a good day in a time trial. If he can do that, why not me?' At the end of September 2014, not long after Jens broke the record, around the time of the world road race championship, I had a sit-down to discuss it with Carsten Jeppesen of Team Sky. Carsten's official job is Head of Technical Operations, but basically he's the man who gets things done, particularly on the equipment side. He was the man who would have to get the bike sorted, and would get the record attempt set up with a date, a venue and so on.

⊙ 'There is no one else to rely on, no one to do it for me. It's just me and the clock. All
the training has been done and now everyone has come to watch me. It feels a bit like
going to the gallows. I want to get on with it. I don't want to sit here any longer. I don't
want to go through another few minutes thinking about it. I'm just ready to go.' ⊙

My Hour was going to be about my personal performance on the day, but I wanted to turn it into something larger than that. It had to be an event; I wanted everyone to go away happy afterwards. That was important. People have done the Hour in so many ways. Obree had about three people there for his first one, while Rominger's first was all but behind closed doors. He took the record first go, and for the second one they got the television cameras in. Merckx's was high-profile, and so was Indurain's in Bordeaux; Boardman's three attempts were all very public, each tied in with major occasions such as the world championships or the Tour. I felt that if I was doing the Hour Record then it should be about pleasing the public as well as about the physical performance – it would be open house with everyone invited, it would be a big event and it would be televised. I didn't ever consider doing it any other way.

Subconsciously I probably needed it to be like that. The bigger the event and the more the date was set in stone, the more motivated I would be to get out of bed in the morning to train and do what was necessary. The challenge wasn't going to be just doing the Hour, it was going to be getting the best out of myself in front of everybody. I wanted to aim for mid-June 2015, although the actual date ended up dependent on the slots Sky Television had available. Sky were coming on board to sponsor Team Wiggins, the new squad I was setting up, which I would be riding for from spring 2015. The television rights to my Hour ride were part of the same package. There was just one problem: by setting it up this way in London rather than in Manchester or elsewhere, I knew that I was giving away maybe a kilometre in terms of the distance I might be able to cover. London is a slower track than Manchester and is at sea level, so you also don't have the benefits that you would gain from an altitude attempt in, say, Mexico City.

There was something else. When I looked at the list of people who have held the Hour Record, there was a little club of five who had won the Tour de France and also held the Hour Record: Lucien Petit-Breton, Fausto Coppi, Jacques Anquetil, Eddy Merckx and Miguel Indurain. I wanted a place on that list and I liked the tradition I would be trying to keep up. If I went for the Hour it would be a throwback to the years when Anquetil, Merckx or Indurain won the biggest bike race in the world and the Hour was what came next. If everything went to plan, it would allow me to put the Hour Record on my CV; I would then be able to compare myself to those greats, using the equipment available to me 20 years on. Maybe I wouldn't manage to get past all their distances, but I could still hold the record. It's like that fastest lap on *Top Gear* – you're not at the top, because some drivers have wet tracks, some don't, but you are up there, still on that list. No one can ever take that away.

Nowadays the record is no longer a rite of passage for a rider who has won the Tour. Of the guys who have won the Tour between Indurain's last win in 1995 and now, I struggle to think of any who would go further than me. That's because riders don't race on the track as much so they don't have the skills, and the Tour is often won by climbers these days rather than time triallists. Perhaps Jan Ullrich of Germany might have managed it in his heyday – he won the Tour in 1997, and was a superb time triallist, taking the world championship in 1999 – and if he raced in the same condition he rode the Tour. But where Jan's chances are concerned, you have to remember that breaking the Hour is not just about producing a certain amount of power but riding the 60 minutes at the perfect pace. It's about the mental ability to maintain discipline for the whole time, and you can't be certain how he would stand up in that department. For example, Evgeni Berzin, who won the Giro d'Italia in 1994, went for it three years later and failed. Chris Froome? It would be good to see how he would do, but, again, his main strength is his climbing. Lance Armstrong? With his pedalling style I can't imagine him riding round a banking. Floyd Landis, Marco Pantani, Alberto Contador, Carlos Sastre or Vincenzo Nibali? I can't see any of those. It's a shame Greg LeMond never did it, though. I'd have loved to have seen him on the boards.

The UCI opened the door for me and the others, so I was in a win-win situation. The Hour definitely fitted into my plans for the end of my career. I'm proud of the fact that I have won major races in so many different disciplines, with the world madison championship, the Olympic pursuit and team pursuit, alongside a Tour de France, a time trial world title and the leader's jerseys in all three Grand Tours. However, that's not something I really chase after. I don't say, 'I'll go for this or that because that's something I've not done before.' It's not as if I'm going to be targeting the cyclo-cross world championship because I've not won a medal there. It's about being capable of doing those things and the opportunity being there in front of me.

When I decided to target Paris–Roubaix in the winter of 2014–15, the motivation wasn't to add it to the list because I was missing one of the Monuments – the name given to the biggest five one-day races. It was just that I've always loved riding Roubaix, and I had a dream of placing highly in it. I thought I'd be able to finish in the top ten, and so we put a whole programme together to build towards doing that. In the event I ran in eighteenth, but that was satisfying enough given that I'd been in a position to win in the finale, which is as much as you can hope for at Roubaix. The Hour was a natural follow-on from my past days on the track – I've won gold medals on the track and I can time-trial, so it was a no-brainer. But there was a little bit of pressure from the cycling world – a feeling of 'They've changed the rules so you've got to do it, Brad. You're a world time trial champion, an Olympic pursuit champion: you're obliged to do it.' To some extent, I felt I had no option but to go for it after the successful attempts that Rohan Dennis and Alex Dowsett had made. If I didn't, people would always have said, 'Why didn't you do it? You'd have got it easily.' But that widespread expectation created pressure as well. It's one thing getting results when you're coming from left field and surprising everyone. When

everyone knows you can win, and should win, you know that defeat will be all the harder to take.

I'm out of the gate, and all the initial questions – how will you feel? how will you manage it? – are being answered. 'Yes, I'm feeling pretty good here, the bike feels good, the position feels good, the crowd are in, it's not too hot in here, I've got a good line, it feels fast, there's no wind, all the doors must be shut, I can hear a girl shouting as I come into the back straight, I wonder if my family are in the track centre, they must be, I saw them earlier.'

I'm focused on the effort but it's quite easy, and because the effort is easy you can think about other things. My mind isn't wavering – yet – and my legs are fresh. I'm just controlling the pace, but I'm having to make myself do it. I've got Heiko Salzwedel, my trainer, standing by the trackside with my lap time on his computer, and that's my guide. After the first few laps, it starts to dawn on me: I'm lapping way faster than the pace I should be riding. I've gone out quite hard, compared to the standing starts I was doing in training on the track during the week. For those practice efforts I'd been starting slowly; it had been taking me a couple of laps to get up to speed. I'd been going out of the blocks really conservatively because Heiko had said, 'Even if it takes you five minutes to get up to pace, it's only ten seconds lost, so who cares – this is an hour-long effort.' Even yesterday, when we did a standing five-kilometre effort, I started quite hard and it took me three or four laps to start seeing the lap time drop to 16.3sec. This feels really easy, but all at once I realise I've left the gate with what I believed to be the same level of effort, but after two laps I'm already down to just over 15sec for a lap. That pace would give me 4min 15sec for a 4,000m pursuit, which is around the Olympic record I set in Beijing in 2008. I can see Heiko waving furiously at me from the trackside: I've got to slow down. It has to be the adrenalin, or maybe the couple of espressos I knocked back before coming up into the track centre.

It's only lap four, and I'm physically lifting my feet off the pedals to bring the pace right back down – whoa, whoa, float round the banking here, break the momentum, like trying to stop a pendulum swinging further than it should – and now I've settled right back in to 16.3sec, which is what I need to break Tony Rominger's record.

That's the first thing I've found out: this is a completely different event on the day compared to how you train. I'm sitting on 16.3sec quite comfortably for a couple of minutes, thinking, 'Sod the high air pressure, I can get Rominger's record, maybe it's still on, this is fine.' I'm constantly weighing up what it feels like, and gradually I start to drift back on to 16.4sec, then to 16.5.

It's clear now: I have to take responsibility for how I pace this. No matter how much training you do, the decision about how you pace it on the day is what makes and breaks the record. I think of people like Jack Bobridge, who went out for 10 or 15 minutes on a pace he couldn't sustain, and finally cracked. The point is that you can't rely on anyone to slow you down in those moments. You have to feel it for yourself: 'Can I keep this up?' That's what makes you good or bad as a time triallist, and ultimately makes you a record holder or someone who falls short. Heiko is my guide, but it's down to me to decide: 'Can I keep this up for 55 more minutes?'

Vikingskipet, Hamar, Norway, 17 July 1993: 51.596km
Vélodrome de Bordeaux Lac, 27 April 1994: 52.713km

Graeme and I have crossed paths several times over the years, but the first time I became aware of the Hour Record was thanks to him. It was in 1993 when he went for it at Herne Hill, the outdoor track in south London where I raced as a kid. I wasn't quite 13 years old and I was at the Good Friday meeting that year even though I didn't know what the Hour was or who Graeme was. He was there spinning round the bumpy concrete between the Golden Wheel sprint rounds and bunched races in that tucked-up position of his on his home-made bike, with the announcer telling us how he was doing.

Obree's story is one of cycling's best-known tales: the lad from Irvine, Scotland, who was flat broke – hunting for 5p coins down the back of the sofa to buy a loaf of bread – but who built his own bike and took on the world. A month or two after that Herne Hill ride, Graeme went for it indoors in Norway, at the track in Hamar – incredibly, he made two attempts in 48 hours – and got it; I can still see that famous photo from afterwards, with his manager Vic Haines and his handful of supporters holding the little board up with the distance chalked on it: 51.596km.

There's a bit more to it than that, though: Graeme's rivalry with Chris Boardman in the British time-trial world made headlines in the mid-nineties, and, later on, when Graeme hit problems with the UCI over his radical aerodynamic riding positions, you couldn't help feeling that here was the little guy with the small budget taking on the sport's blazers. And off the bike it's not been an easy ride: Graeme suffered from depression, made several suicide attempts, and came out a few years ago, which is a rare thing for any sportsman to do. He has never given up on cycling though, and the films and books about his life story are well worth taking a look at.

At Herne Hill on a blustery spring day on 9 April 1993 he was riding on an outdoor track at sea level, but he was going for Francesco Moser's Record, set at altitude in

*Obree celebrating breaking the
record in an empty velodrome in
Norway in 1993*

Mexico City on a massive budget with extensive technical support. In the end, Graeme did 49.381km, which was only 50m short of Eddy Merckx's record. You had to be there to understand what it meant – I was barely into my teens, I'd just started racing a bike, I had a vague idea of who the big names were and then, all of a sudden, you come across this ordinary-looking bloke riding a bike in a way you've never seen before, and getting up there with legendary figures like Merckx and Moser. That's romance. And it's inspirational: if Graeme – a rider who rode races I knew about like the national '25', and raced at Herne Hill as well – could do it, why not a kid like me?

⦿ 'By halfway, it felt like hell . . . Minutes seemed like hours . . . Many times, I
thought about how nice it would be to stop and end the agony. I was up on the
record, though, and I would go on and on . . . even if I had to ride to death by
exhaustion . . . and every lap I thought about the failure . . . I was in agony by the
last quarter of the ride: my feet, ankles, genitals, hands, face and scalp had all
gone completely numb.' ⦿ **Graeme Obree**

17 minutes

DRIVING YOURSELF
SLOWLY CRAZY

In the first ten minutes of an Hour attempt, you're still fresh and it's relatively straightforward. It feels almost effortless – not exactly easy, because I'm travelling at 55km/h – but early on it shouldn't be hurting if I am hoping to sustain this for an hour. I keep backing off, almost letting the pedals go round by themselves, but then I come round to where Heiko is standing, and find I have gone a tenth of a second faster.

Previous page: *Training ride on Sa Calobra in Majorca*

I wonder where that's come from, then I wonder what all these people are thinking; I can hear them shouting, I can almost hear the individual voices; I can hear Hugh Porter commentating. I'm really spatially aware. The tunnel vision will come when the effort truly starts kicking in. For now, I think I can take on the world, but later it is bound to catch up with me a bit.

I haven't got the total focus that it takes to ride a prologue time trial or a pursuit and I'm aware of so much. There are all sorts of things going through my head early on, certain voices I can hear, and there's one that sticks in my mind: the sound of a girl aged about ten, just on the entrance to the home straight, really screaming at the top of her voice, 'G'won, Bradley', in a real Cockney accent. I wonder who it is.

I look at Heiko's screen every lap, and I'll glance at the clock every so often. 'Right, I've done seven minutes, now that's fine . . . I've done eight minutes now. I'm ticking them off.'

I had been sitting around all week in a hotel in Soho waiting for this. The final block of training in Majorca lasted three weeks, putting in the workload on the slow track in Palma where the 2007 world championships were held. We flew back after our final session on

the Friday, nine days before the record. I had the weekend at home in Lancashire then travelled down to London on the Sunday night; seven days to go. I spent most of the week putting in one- or two-hour rides around Regent's Park in the morning – it's about three miles round, so it takes about five minutes per lap – before going to do a session on the track at Lee Valley VeloPark in the evening.

It all felt very much as if I'd come back to where I began. As a kid, I'd raced regularly at Herne Hill outdoor track and the Eastway Cycle Circuit; Eastway was on the site where the Olympic velodrome is now – when you stand outside the door you can still see the same London skyline you would look at from the circuit's only hill – and I started off riding my bike round Regent's Park as a kid, all on my own with no other cyclists there apart from the odd courier. It was brilliant riding around the park – the number of cyclists was unbelievable. Almost 25 years later I was back attempting one of the last things I'll do in my career, riding around Regent's Park again, this time with hordes of cyclists, all doing double takes, asking, 'Is that Brad?' I'd have a bit of a chat to one or two of them – 'Oh, when are you going for this record then?', that kind of thing – but really I was just doing what everyone else was doing.

Everything built towards Wednesday evening when the plan was to do a half-distance dress rehearsal at the track. The idea was that I would go in and have everything set up as if it was race day, go at full pace for 30 minutes and then go again for another 15 minutes. For the first half-hour I went at pretty much the same average speed that I did on the day, and found it fairly easy, so I came away from it feeling confident – 'That's fine, I've only got half an hour longer to do on the day, and I felt OK at half distance' – and we dropped the other 15-minute block. When race day came it was reassuring to know that three days before I had found the speed no problem over half the distance I wanted to cover.

On Thursday we got in the car and drove out of London to Denham, where I used to go as a kid to meet a chain gang – a fast evening ride run by the local road racers – which met at Denham Nurseries near Uxbridge. I headed off on the route that we used to do – towards Marlow and Henley through Burnham Beeches, Beaconsfield, out where they used to route the Archer Grand Prix, an international one-day race that dated back to 1956 and lasted until 2007. Riding those roads took me back, and was a bit of escapism, a way of getting out of that daily routine and clearing my head. It also felt a little like a pilgrimage, as I hadn't ridden on those roads for nearly 20 years. We did three hours, finished at Henley, then drove back into London.

Friday was a day off. On Saturday we weren't on the track until the evening and that was just a standing start and five minutes on record pace, just a tickler to open up my system. There was one event of note, however: our aerodynamics specialist, Dimitris Katsanis, said, 'If I was you, I'd get rid of that beard', so that had to go – and I felt naked without it. It was one of those things. You start putting it all together, I'd shaved my head a few weeks earlier – it's not so much the aerodynamics, but the commitment, knowing you've done everything you can. It was game time. It wasn't a fashion show.

On Sunday it was a matter of getting ready. It felt like I'd been building up for months on end, and in particular the last couple of weeks. I'd finally got there, it was 7 June at last. It was all quite relaxed: I went and did a little ride on the turbo in the hotel in the morning; all my friends and family were staying in the hotel, so they were wandering about, excited, hungover from the night before. I kept bumping into people as I went through my routine; I was eating my chicken and rice – standard pre-race food, nothing fancy – in the restaurant at lunchtime while they were propping up the bar next door, putting back the gin and tonics.

With a time trial there is always an element of concern. There is stuff you have to keep in your mind: 'I've got to remember that corner. What about that drain cover? I hope it doesn't rain – what's the weather looking like?' For this one, I knew exactly what I had

Left: *I have my children's names tattooed on my arm, and their initials on the backs of my hands so that I can see them when I'm in my time-trial postion.*
Right: *With my wife, Cath, on the morning of the ride*

to do, exactly what pace I'd be riding. I'd been over it hundreds and hundreds of times, I'd been through lap after lap after lap in training on the pace I had to do so it was embedded in me, ingrained in me. We'd planned it for so long that it all seemed normal. Once I'd got to the velodrome, I went down to the track to have a quick look, to soak up the atmosphere, then went back to the little room behind the track where I was to warm up. It was quite a relaxing thing to go and do. Once I started warming up I just dialled in to the focus. It was the sort of effort where you have to be relaxed at the start; I could almost ride in my sleep at the intensity you ride at early on.

We didn't plan for me to ride to my seven-minute 'platforms of hope', but we could be forgiven for that:

we had been shooting in the dark when we started the build-up. When I started looking ahead to the record with my back-up team there was no one we could turn to who knew how to train for an Hour. I did the obvious thing and spoke to Chris Boardman, but we didn't get any real insights because he rode his first off the back of riding the British time-trial calendar, and the second after the Tour de France; I was coming to it from a Classics campaign with Team Sky – my body was in a totally different state. Heiko had never trained any of his riders for an Hour, and Tim Kerrison – the physiologist who helped me win the Tour, and gave us a hand on that side of this project – was in the same boat. I had only seven weeks to play with and the question was: what do you do in that time? What kind of training is best? There is no point in going to Majorca and going up and down Lluc or Puig Major when you are going to ride on the track.

We found a way into it from a copy of *Cycle Sport* magazine I'd bought in 1994, when I was 14, and Miguel Indurain had recently broken the record. I just happened to come across it; the article goes through everything Miguel did, his full diary from finishing the Tour on 23 July up to taking the Hour Record on 2 September. The timescale he had to work within wasn't that different from mine. His training on the Bordeaux track consisted mainly of ten-kilometre blocks, a distance that is not too long and not too short; he built up to five ten-kilometre blocks, so I thought that was a good place to start.

BUILDING AN HOUR RECORD

1 **Aero helmet** – same as the one I used for the time trial in London 2012, sprayed gold.

2 **Skinsuit** – designed by Rapha to minimise drag.

3 **Chain** – standard Dura-Ace chain treated specifically for the attempt to reduce friction. The cost of development was £6,000, making it the most expensive bike chain in the world.

4 **Gearing** – a 58x14 ratio was chosen on the day to keep my cadence at 105RPM for the attempt. The chain ring was built specifically for the record attempt by the highly-skilled precision engineers at Hope Technology. The higher air pressure meant that I was forced to take a smaller gear than I had originally planned to keep my cadence and power output in check.

5 **Frame** – Pinarello worked with Jaguar to develop the Bolide HR bike, improving the aero efficiency by 7.5 per cent compared with the road-going version of the model.

6 **Power** – my aerobic threshold is between 420 watts and 460 watts. During the record I would have to average 440 watts to hit my 55km target.

7 **Handlebars** – 3D printed and made out of titanium, these handlebars were built to support my precise time-trial position.

AIR PRESSURE

As the air pressure increases, so does the power needed to push the air out of the way. So high air pressure means lower speed and therefore shorter distances. For every 20 millibar increase in air pressure, the lap time goes up by about 0.1 seconds. The chart below shows how this affects the final distance travelled.

AIR PRESSURE (in Mb)	955	975	995	1015	1035	1055
LAPS	224	222	221	219	218	217
AVERAGE LAP TIME	16.1	16.2	16.3	16.4	16.5	16.6
DISTANCE	55,880	55,535	55,195	54,858	54,526	54,198

The record had been in the back of my mind while I was building up to Paris–Roubaix. I couldn't help keeping a bit of an eye on various attempts to go further than the Austrian Matthias Brändle, who had beaten Jens Voigt's record at the end of October 2014. In January Jack Bobridge went for it and failed, whereas I'd expected him to go a long way. When we were at the Tour of Qatar in February, Rohan Dennis made his attempt, and got past Brändle's distance, but he only managed 52.491km, which wasn't as far as I thought he would go, so that was reassuring.

There were a couple of other attempts in February and March by Thomas Dekker and Gustav Larsson, both unsuccessful, but it was my fellow Briton Alex Dowsett – an ex-GB academy rider and a seriously good time triallist – who eventually raised the bar five weeks before I was due to go. When Alex went for the record on 2 May, I was racing at the Tour de Yorkshire with Team Wiggins, which was my first race after Paris–Roubaix. We were actually riding the second stage while he was doing it. I felt sure he'd break the record but he went further than I thought he'd go, with 52.937km – we'd seen what Rohan Dennis was capable of and I knew that Rohan wasn't a pushover. I watched Alex on YouTube afterwards – he looked really languid and effortless for the first 40 minutes. He had a whopping big gear on so you never got the impression of speed; he just looked totally in control, keeping a good line on the track.

Apart from Alex, who appeared to have invested a lot of time in it, all the other guys looked as if they'd just kicked on from their normal road programme – won a stage in the Tour Down Under or something, then just got on the track and had a go. I wanted to allow a bit more time than they had done, to make sure I gave myself the chance to do it properly. I was confident that I could manage 53km quite easily. That was no disrespect to Alex, it was what I felt I could do. Had the record been at 54.5, that might have influenced the decision as to whether I took it on or not.

After finishing Roubaix I had a week off then I went to the track at Manchester to start training. Paul Manning, one of the Great Britain coaches – and a former teammate from the team pursuit days – was taking the session; I told him about Indurain and the ten-kilometre blocks, so we did five ten-kilometre blocks just to get an idea of whether I could ride at that pace. That's where we started from. We adapted those sessions, went a bit longer, up to 15km – just to see what 53km/h felt like. The big question when it came to the training was how to break the whole thing down, rather than working in terms of one hour. In training you are looking to go for 10 or 20 minutes at the speed you want rather than going for an hour and seeing what you can do. Once you've established the speed, you try to build up the time so you can sustain the speed for 60 minutes. Six 10-minute blocks seemed too many; if you try four 15-minute blocks each one will be too long, so I came to like the idea of five 12-minute blocks. That gave us a structure for training – each 12-minute block is just over ten kilometres, it's about 11min 20sec for ten kilometres.

⊙ 'I knew exactly what I had to do, exactly what pace I'd
be riding. I'd been over it hundreds of and hundreds of
times, I'd been through lap after lap after lap in training
on the pace I had to do so it was embedded in me,
ingrained in me.' ⊙

*Training started on the Manchester
Velodrome*

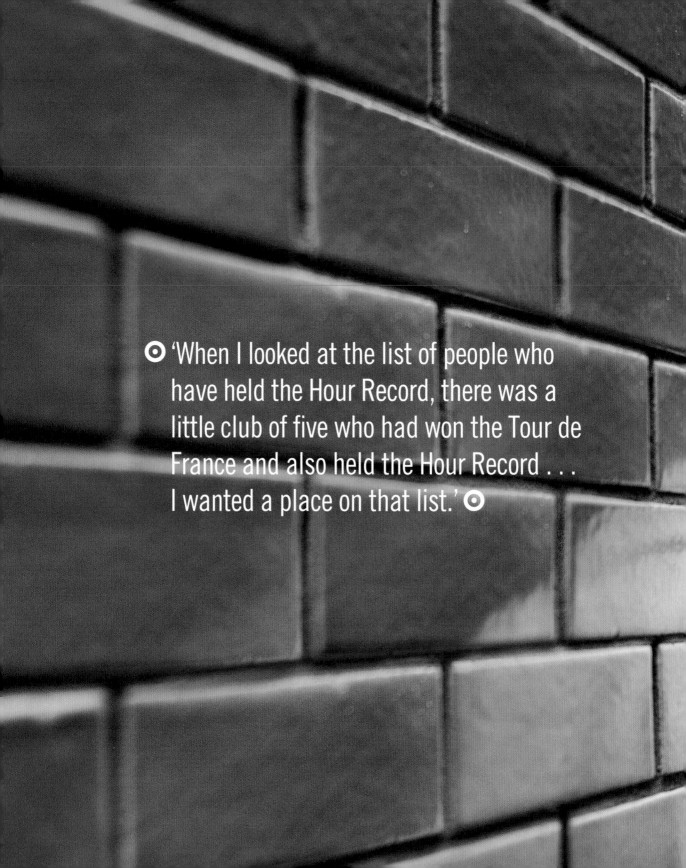

⊙ 'When I looked at the list of people who have held the Hour Record, there was a little club of five who had won the Tour de France and also held the Hour Record . . . I wanted a place on that list.' ⊙

*On the cobbles of Paris-Roubaix
in April 2015*

The training all stemmed from that. You work a lot around the first 12 minutes from the standing start, repeating those, and then maybe doubling up, so we'd do two 24-minute blocks, then 36 minutes. It was really number-oriented, quantifiable, clinical. It's all numbers with the Hour – you have to hit this lap time, this power output, this time for five or ten kilometres, this average speed. Everything comes down to the numbers. Compared to the road, there are relatively few variables, apart from the air pressure, and you adjust the schedule and the gearing according to that. On the day, I realised when I went out on the track that a 55.2km pace was not going to be achievable given the weather conditions, so I just backed off by 0.2sec per lap to 54.5km.

We didn't really get into the swing of it until after Paris–Roubaix. The initial discussion with Carsten in September 2014 was more about the bike and the date. After that we didn't give it any thought other than to tell the people who were going to organise it that I could do it next year, this was the date, this was the venue, and we wanted to make a big event of it. Then it was a question of letting them get on with it as I focused on the road and trying to win Paris–Roubaix. The only idea I had six months out was, because it was a celebration of the Hour, to try and present all the former record holders on the track that day – Eddy Merckx, Chris Boardman, Francesco Moser, Miguel Indurain, Graeme Obree – but when you contact them it's not so simple.

Merckx couldn't come because he was doing a Gran Fondo, a big long-distance event in Italy. Boardman was commentating for television at the Dauphiné Libéré. In the end, Indurain came off his own bat, paying his own way, and some major figures who you wouldn't normally see at a bike race came too – Seb Coe, for example, and the England Rugby World Cup-winning captain Martin Johnson. I'd asked for Hugh Porter to do the announcements in the velodrome as I think he's brilliant at relaying to the public what they are seeing, and also because it was Hugh who was commentating for television when I won my first Olympic gold medal in Athens. He's the best at explaining cycling to people who don't know the ins and outs, especially track cycling, and I knew we'd have a lot of first-time viewers. The event organisers did a great job, with a full schedule of build-up races to keep the public entertained before I got on the boards.

In terms of training, we'd do those blocks of 12 minutes, and repeated blocks. We were training on the Manchester Velodrome and during the late spring we were getting some really fast times back, over 55km/h. We knew London would be just a little bit slower than Manchester – I've never worked out why; I think it may be that you exit the bankings differently due to a slightly different design – but for what we wanted the event to be, and because of the Olympic connection, it had to be London. We also travelled to Palma to train on a slower track, to make it more of a slog. That's one of Heiko's principles: train heavy, race light. It all makes you feel better come race day, like training on the track on spoked wheels and putting in your disc wheel at the last moment.

Training in Manchester. When we
started out it's fair to say that
none of us knew how to prepare
for an event of this sort. There are
no books you can read and few
experts to consult

London is a slower track than Manchester, under the same barometric conditions, but that's not the whole story. If you examine atmospheric pressure, as we had to, it usually seems to be higher in London than in Manchester. It's because of the Pennines, so they tell me, the way Manchester is located. It's critical, because the higher the air pressure the more power you need to produce to push yourself and the bike through the air; that can be like the difference between riding on a gravelly track and a smooth Majorcan tarmac road, trying to sustain 30mph. The Great Britain cycling performance director, Shane Sutton, who had been helping with the training, calls it 'riding in treacle'. Another GB coach, Iain Dyer, said it was like going through custard.

For every 20 millibars the air pressure goes up, your lap time increases by 0.1sec. For example, in Manchester I had been travelling at 55km/h in training, which roughly equated to Tony Rominger's second record; on days when the pressure was 990 millibars I'd do 30 minutes at 55km/h putting out 410 watts. My aerobic threshold is between 420 and 460 watts, so putting out that power I could have kept going at that pace for an hour and a half. That was why we started working towards the 55km target. In London on the day, however, because the air pressure was 1,036 millibars, to cover 54.5km in the hour I had to average 440 watts; to stick to that 55km/h schedule would have taken 460 watts, which I couldn't sustain. The pace I went depended on the pressure on the day. The difference can be huge – when Chris did his hour in 1996 he had something like 955 millibars.

In the final run-in to the record on 7 June, the air pressure was the only thing I had to worry about. We were monitoring the weather all week, and the millibars just kept on going up and up and up. I sat there watching weather websites, figuring out what the pressure was going to be, calculating what each increase would mean in terms of lost distance. I got to the point where I knew there was nothing I could do about it and I was just going to have to go for it. On the day when I got to the track and sat down with Shane and Heiko, two hours before I was going to start, we talked it through and realised the pressure was so high – it had increased by 10 or 20 millibars since the dress rehearsal on the Wednesday – that I would have to ride on a slightly lower gear, because I would lose so much speed.

I was working on a cadence of 105 revs per minute, which Heiko, Shane and I felt was the optimum cadence for one hour: the best for me, for that distance. Pedalling at that speed gives you a little bit of wriggle room either way. It's big enough to get some momentum at the start in the first half an hour, but low enough to give some security in the last 15 minutes when you don't want to become bogged down on the gear. That's one of the key things: if you are tailing off before the end, and you are going to blow, you can't change gear. So it's important to pick the right gear before you start. Dropping the gear on the day meant I would have a bit to play with when it got tough in the finale.

The plan was to stick with a similar cadence whatever the distance we went for, adjusting the gearing so that I'd still be pedalling at almost the same rate but travelling at a slightly slower speed.

If I'd had normal air pressure for that time of year – 1,000 millibars – I would have gone over 600m further. It was the difference between 16.2 and 16.4sec per lap. It doesn't sound a lot, but when you are on the boards it's huge; if I had set out on the day trying to ride 16.1sec laps when the pressure was only suitable for 16.4sec, the extra power I would have needed would have been massive. So when you are on the track, you have to be really calculating and tell yourself, 'You're going to have to be sensible here: just rein it in a little bit.'

I'm looking at the clock, seeing 51 minutes left, and thinking, 'Good, that's nine minutes down, but you're going to have to start focusing, Brad. You've got to stop clock-watching, concentrate on the effort. It's going to get hard now.' So I start talking to myself. I'm looking up again, thinking, 'Ten minutes has gone now. OK, that took quite a long time to go that ten minutes.' Gradually I can feel the effort and I start wondering, 'Can I sustain this from A to B?' I've gone through the initial bit where it feels easy and I'm starting to think more realistically now. And listening to my body, it's now that I start realising this feels all right but it is going to get hard.

After 15 minutes I begin to tell myself, 'You can't think about that girl shouting in the corner. You've got to start focusing: think about pedalling out of the banking, keep looking at Heiko, watch those splits.' That starts to come into play more and more – 'Right, seventeen minutes in now, got to start focusing; another three minutes and that's twenty minutes. You'll only have ten minutes then until you're halfway. How will that feel, when you get to halfway?'

Agustin Melgar Velodrome, Mexico City, 25 October 1972: 49.431km

When we race at the Tour of Qatar, we stay in the Sheraton Hotel, which has several different levels and a view down into the lobby. When I was there in February 2015, Eddy came out of the lift and started chatting to me – 'Where are you going to do the Hour, when are you going to do it?' He asked me the date because he wanted to come, but in the end he couldn't make it. I remember him telling me, 'The best place to do it is Stuttgart', because the longer straights give you more speed. Apparently it was Francesco Moser who noticed this. Eddy was set on me doing it in Stuttgart, but I was always going to ride it in London. Other than that, I remember him saying, 'There is only you who can do it; Tony Martin' – the world time trial champion – 'can't do it, because he needs to change his position'. Talking to Eddy Merckx about the Hour is one of those things you savour as a cycling fan.

I love Eddy: I've got the jersey he was wearing when he won Ghent–Wevelgem in 1973 – Molteni-Arcore, with the original numbers on – and one of his bikes from 1976. And not long after I'd finished my Hour, my wife Cath and I went to the Merckx exhibition in Brussels that was set up by his friend the racing driver Jacky Ickx. We just went as fans, not as guests, and I was blown away by the stuff they'd pulled together for it.

In some ways I think the Merckx Hour Record from 1972 – Mexico City, 49.431km – is the stand-out one. Chris Boardman did an Athlete's Hour on what was meant to be the same kit as Eddy, but even then his set-up didn't totally replicate what Eddy used – Chris had a filled helmet where Eddy had a hairnet crash-hat, Chris wore overshoes, and had a skinsuit where Merckx had woolly kit. Everything about Merckx's 49.431km is incredible. Growing up I was always aware of Merckx – you couldn't help hearing about him from

⊙'I had no moments of weakness, but it never felt easy. The Hour demands a total, permanent, intense effort which is in a class of its own. I will never do another. There are other races to get on my record, but I've achieved what I need now. You can't conceive of a great career without the Hour.' ⊙ **Eddy Merckx**

Eddy Merckx in Mexico City set the benchmark by which all other Hour records are measured

older cyclists as his era was only 20 years before I began. I probably heard about his Hour in my teens when I watched a video called *Cycling's Greatest Moments*, presented by Phil Liggett. It included clips of cycling films like *Stars and Watercarriers* and *A Sunday in Hell*, along with great Tour moments like Greg LeMond beating Laurent Fignon by 8sec in 1989 – it was a round-up of the legendary stories, and of course Eddy's Hour was in there.

Merckx's Hour was the definitive record. He's the benchmark. I've spoken about going for the record again and I'm toying with going for his distance in an Athlete's Hour of my own. I'm planning on doing some tests with similar kit – a hairnet crash-hat and so on – to see what the numbers are. I might be way off his pace. I might not be able to hold his position and be as aerodynamic, but then Merckx wasn't aero in the slightest. You watch him riding it and he's all over the place. You compare him with Chris doing his Athlete's Hour and Chris is so aerodynamic with that hunched back. In some ways that just makes Merckx's even better. He starts so fast. He did the first five kilometres in 5min 55sec, which would have got him a medal in a world pursuit championship at the time; he breaks the 5, 10 and 20km records which Ole Ritter set in a special ride which wasn't an Hour. And he just grunts it out for an hour with sheer brute force.

Vélodrome de Bordeaux Lac, 22 October 1994: 53.832km
Vélodrome de Bordeaux Lac, 5 November 1994: 55.291km

The benchmark distance that stuck in my mind through the build-up to 7 June was 55.291km, which was the record set by Tony Rominger in Bordeaux on Guy Fawkes Night,1994. It was the kind of distance we were getting on certain days in Manchester when the training went well and the air pressure was relatively low, so it became a goal that might just have been possible for me to reach in the right conditions, whereas – as I've said before – the ultimate distance set by Chris Boardman using the Superman position in 1996 always looked out of the question unless something exceptional happened. Chris's record was out there in a position that I couldn't use any more, but Rominger was the one I fixated on because that was in a position that resembled the one I rode in.

Like Miguel Indurain's Hour a month or so earlier, Rominger's record was a classic case of a rider just getting on the track after his road season, picking up some technique and seeing what he could do. It was also masterminded by Dr Michele Ferrari, who is now infamous as Lance Armstrong's trainer, but back then had been Rominger's trainer since the early 1990s and was just known as an Italian doctor who'd said something unfortunate about EPO. Tony was the second-best stage racer of the early nineties, behind Indurain; that year he'd won the Vuelta for the third year running, and had just won the Grand Prix des Nations and Grand Prix Eddy Merckx, both classic time trials which are now defunct.

Tony hadn't ever been on a track, and he fell off the first time he got on the boards; but he then took a couple of days getting used to the bankings before going for the record proper on 22 October, behind closed doors, in what boiled down to a dress rehearsal with officials present. They then went away and tweaked the bike – which had

*Tony Rominger had so
little track experience
when he first attempted
the Hour that he fell off
during practice*

I felt Rominger's distance of 55.291km was in the realms of possibility for me

handlebars designed by Dr Ferrari himself, according to his website – and came back for the real thing 13 days later. He added over two kilometres to Miguel's record – he did 4min 24sec for the first four kilometres, which would have won him the world pursuit championship that year – but if you think how much smaller and more aerodynamic he was, and how much less weight he was shoving round the bankings, that all adds up.

If you look at the people who've gone for the Hour twice, they've tended to go faster the second time. That's not always the case, however – Indurain tried again, in Bogotá in 1995 after the world road championships in Colombia, and he didn't finish. He won the time trial and got second in the road race and went a week later, the idea being that he would go further at altitude, but it didn't work out like that. Rominger did it again and went further, so did Chris and Graeme Obree. As for Moser, he just kept on doing the Hour. Doing the Hour for the first time is always going to be harder, because you have to learn how to pace it, and you have absolutely nothing to go from: the Hour is simply unique. But if you've got enough in you to do it again, you should usually go faster.

27 minutes

DIGGING IN

The Hour is all about the clock ticking away. 'The demonic clock', Fausto Coppi called it. It's actually an electronic display in the track, but it's still the key point of reference for the crowd, for the commentators, and it's vital for me as well. And here there's a bit of gamesmanship. I want to play with my mind. For Rohan Dennis's attempt the clock counted upwards – for mine it's counting down. The idea is that I will always keep thinking the glass is half full rather than half empty: I'll end up keeping my spirits afloat by thinking, 'There's only 25 minutes to go now', or 'Ten minutes from now there's going to be 15 minutes to go.' The only thing is the clock goes to 59 straight away, so when it is showing zero I'll actually still have a minute to do.

Previous page: *The trick is to pedal slightly harder as you enter the banking, that way you can keep your power effort as smooth as possible throughout the lap*

With Heiko's computer showing me the lap splits, and telling me how far I am projected to go, and the clock giving me an idea of how much time I have left, there's only one thing remaining for me to do: I have to try to get into a mental zone where I'm only concentrating on my pedalling through each banking. The point is that when you are riding the track you're not just giving it your all as you fly round and round. A few journalists tried to do Hour Records of their own around the time I did mine, to get some idea of what's involved, but it's not just a case of riding as hard as you can, like sitting on a turbo trainer. It takes a fair degree of skill.

Each time you go through one of the bankings you speed up a little because you are going slightly downhill. You have to match that with your cadence, and try and profit from the impetus you pick up by pedalling a bit more to maximise what you take out of the banking. So as you get sling-shot out of the banking on to the straight, you almost back off – not a huge amount, not sitting up – but with a feel that you acquire once you've done it enough times: squeeze on the pedals in the banking,

normal in the straight, squeeze in the banking, normal in the straight. If you didn't do that your power graph would be up and down the whole way through, like an Alpine stage profile – the idea is to keep the power consistent throughout: by pedalling slightly harder in the bankings you're keeping the power up and gaining speed. If you do it in the straight it's counter-productive; you're not going any faster but you're using more power, so you might as well use the power in the bankings, which are the fastest point of the track.

So I focus on doing that during the ride and match that pattern with the lap splits I'm seeing on Heiko's screen, then compare both of those again with my effort. It means I'm juggling these three things constantly: pedal-banking, pedal-straight, pedal-banking, pedal-straight; look at Heiko: 16.3. Banking, straight, banking, straight, 16.4sec, banking, straight, banking, straight, 16.5sec, banking, straight, 16.3sec, how am I feeling? Banking, straight, banking, straight, 16.4sec, how are my legs?

Perhaps the most important thing that needs to be decided for an Hour Record attempt is how you are going to receive information on the day. You have no computer on your bike, no power meter or pulse monitor, so that data is going to be absolutely critical in deciding how you will pace the ride. Almost always when you ride a timed event on the track, your coach is standing trackside, telling you how you are faring compared to your schedule, but precisely how he feeds you the info is the key thing. Some coaches 'walk the line' – they walk towards the start/finish line or away from it depending on whether you are up or down on time.

It's the simplest way to do it. Chris Boardman told me that the way his coach Peter Keen used to 'walk the line' was that he'd start at the pursuit line – the line marked precisely halfway down each straight, where you start and finish a pursuit, which, confusingly, isn't always the same as the start/finish line – and he'd walk away each lap by however much Chris was up on the record. So if he walked five steps Chris was five seconds up. But the trouble with 'walking the line' was that I was hoping to smash the record. When Chris broke it in 1996 by nearly 1.2km, Pete walked four laps; if we had done it that way, Heiko would have ended up walking nearly seven laps on the day. And, more importantly, I'd probably have lost count of the laps.

Instead, the performance analysts devised a system which would feed back each lap split to Heiko's iPad. That meant that I would be able to see the splits almost in real time; the timing system would put up my exact lap split on the screen, half a lap or about 8sec after I completed each lap. I would hit the timing strip in the back straight and then as I came into the home straight I would get the split from just before. We programmed

The black line around the track marks 250 metres, so you want to be as close to that as possible at all times, without going over it and into the 'Côte d'Azur'

it so that every ten minutes or so it would display my projected distance so I could check it as I passed; for example, it would say if you carry on at this pace you're on 54.6km.

I told the press I'd break the Hour down into the same 12-minute blocks that we had used in training. Breaking it down like that had worked really well; it had helped me compartmentalise the whole thing. The first 12-minute block is almost free, because you are pushed on by the adrenalin from the start and it's a relatively easy pace. You can forget about the last 12 minutes because by that point you've had enough and you are just hanging on and counting down. That just comes naturally from all the training, and is something you can't replicate. You are left with 36 minutes in the middle, which doesn't sound like too much. That's the mid-point, where you have got to be disciplined and hold the pace.

On the day it's a different experience. When you

actually get into the arena and it's a full house with TV cameras and the atmosphere is buzzing, things like that go out of the window. Under those circumstances, I go into race mode. I end up with a completely different focus in the same way that I do with events like major time trials, Olympic finals and so on. You either thrive off that or you don't. You either have the self-control to concentrate on your pace and what your body is telling you, or you don't.

It was that focus that enabled me to back off the 16.2sec lap splits I was hitting early on, which is 55km pace. I had enough control to slow down slightly; I brought it back to 16.4sec and 16.5sec each lap because I realised early on that it was going to get quite tough with the air pressure and so on. That's where experience on those big occasions comes into play and in some ways I pat myself on the back for getting that right because that is what it's all about.

I forgot about the 12-minute idea once I started focusing on the actual effort, on the constant process of figuring out what I was feeling and referring that back to what Heiko's computer screen was telling me from the side of the track. I'd be looking for 16.4sec per lap. If I squeezed too much on one banking because my concentration had wavered a little bit, I'd come round and see 16.1, then I'd just back off slightly. You're constantly doing that throughout the ride.

Previous page: *My trainer Heiko Salzwedel holds the iPad which shows my lap splits and projected distance*

⊙ 'At all other races, there are other people around you to reassure you, even if you don't talk to them, just because you know they are going through exactly the same things as you. If you are racing up a climb and it starts to hurt, you can be sure that other people are in the same boat. With the Hour, however, there are no other people with you and you've got no reference points.' ⊙

That's a skill in itself. It's what makes you good at riding the track in an individual pursuit, and obviously it's what I brought from my background in doing that since I was a junior: you end up able to judge your pace while riding at close to breaking point. There are some cyclists who just can't do that. To take one example, if you watch Tony Rominger's record on YouTube he's constantly wavering by about half a second per lap on some splits. Thomas Dekker did the same; his graph is up and down through the whole ride.

In the last few minutes of the Hour you're just hanging on – but in that you're no different from any other cyclist at the limit of what he or she can do. Cycling is quite a pure sport in that sense: it is mainly about suffering, whether you are climbing the Tourmalet, racing up Mont Ventoux, trying to survive in Paris–Roubaix, or doing a club ten-mile time trial on your local course. You're just trying to hang on to a pace.

When you're chasing the Hour, there are additional external things. Suffering is one thing, but compared to simply putting your head down and going for it up a climb, when you are on a track you've got to keep your form. You've got sandbags inches away from you on the left that you can't hit and you're focusing on that black line around the bottom of the track that you are trying to follow. You've got to ride in a very smooth way. That's part of the reason why a lot of other riders who are physically capable of taking on the Hour will never do it, because they are just not able to adapt to riding the track. That's why I don't think Lance would ever have managed to do it, because he had that stabbing style when he pressed on the pedals.

As well as focusing on the pedalling, when I actually got going I started listening to my body a lot more than I had in training. It was those three things – Heiko's computer screen, the constant banking/straight, pressure on/pressure off, and what my body was telling me. The clock was a fourth factor, although I didn't exactly concentrate on it: every now and then I'd look at it for reference. The key thing was to focus on those three things and avoid looking at the clock too often, as that breaks your concentration. That was quite easy to manage to start with; after a few minutes the effort would start to bite a bit, I'd feel, 'It's starting to hurt a bit now,' and as I thought that I'd look at the clock.

The longer the ride went on, the shorter the time I was able to keep my mind on the three things, so I ended up checking the clock more and more often. The point is that it is not a flat-out effort, like a pursuit where you are so focused for four minutes that you forget everything, and it's not like a time trial where you get bits with no one on the course and nothing to look at. The only other occasion when I've raced for that length of time with that degree of intense focus was the Olympic time trial. It's relentless and it's at a pace where you are able to think so you can't help but waver mentally.

The Hour was tough physically, but what got to me mentally was watching that countdown, minute by minute. I saw that timer every 16 seconds, lap after lap. That just

My kids, Ben and Bella, cheering me on. It's a massive boost knowing they are there on the day to support me

underlines how lonely the Hour is. At all other races, even in a time trial, there are other people around you to reassure you, even if you don't talk to them, just because you know they are going through exactly the same things as you. If you are racing up a climb and it starts to hurt, you can be sure that other people are in the same boat. With the Hour, however, there are no other people with you and you've got no reference points.

Even at a time trial in the Tour or Olympic Games, you are watching other people warming up and going up the start ramp to go through the same things as you. You are still sharing that experience. You take reassurance from that. You can say to yourself, 'Just imagine how they are feeling; I'm really confident.' But when you are doing the Hour, there is no one else. It's just you on that track with 6,000 people who have come to see you succeed or fail.

As I got into the last ten minutes those three things became harder and harder to concentrate on. The banking/straight thing became so monotonous that I'd start wavering, my lap splits would start fluctuating as the fatigue set in and I looked at the lap board and forgot about the three things. You don't see it from trackside, but when you are doing it it becomes tense. In a funny way, it was like driving yourself slowly crazy.

As well as the air pressure, the other thing we couldn't really control was the temperature, although we did try to keep it in check. You need warm air as it's easier to push through, because the air molecules move about more as they heat up, but obviously you don't want it too hot because if your core body temperature gets too high you are in trouble. We wanted it at 27 degrees, but the building ended up getting to 30 degrees, with the crowd in there. During the attempt, we didn't know that was happening; it was only afterwards that we found out. It was hotter than was physically pleasant.

The heat meant that I was getting quite dehydrated as well towards the end. When that happens, you just can't sustain the effort – but I think it was supposed to be like that. If you pace it so that you are getting absolutely everything out, you shouldn't be physically able to ramp it up in the way that Alex did towards the end of his record. What that tells me is that I used up everything I had in me on that day for that ride.

The scientists told me afterwards that as well as raising the temperature, all these people in that confined space end up depriving you of oxygen; there's only so much oxygen in the air and if 6,000 people are breathing it in there is less of it to go round. So going for the Hour in a sold-out velodrome is actually counter-productive to what I was trying to achieve, if you look at it purely in terms of distance covered in the 60 minutes.

The conditions ended up going against me which is why the effort was tailing off a bit in the last ten minutes if you look at the graph. From ten to five minutes to go I slowed down a little, mainly because I was getting uncomfortable on the saddle so I was moving around a bit, and perhaps also because I was saving something for a sprint at the end – which I always like to do. It happened without me really noticing it.

The graph shows that the lap speeds slowed down a little and then I picked up again. In fact, I think I got it just right – I'd rather have been up against it in the final minutes than have had the speed go up dramatically at the end. I was right at my limit – another five minutes and I'd have really started drifting off the pace. I wouldn't have wanted it to be any longer. In terms of riding from A to B for an hour as fast as I could I got it spot on.

When I compare my record and Alex's, it seems as if I had a lower gear on, although it may just have been that I was pedalling faster. Alex's record looks like a completely different race, perhaps because he rode at a pace dictated by the record distance. There was a difference in the way each of us approached the record, in that I think he was unsure whether he'd get it or not and wasn't certain how hard it was going to be.

'It's just you on that track with 6,000 people who have come to see you succeed or fail.'

I had no idea how hard it would be in the last 15 minutes, but I wasn't calculating the ride according to Alex's distance, I was aiming at a target I'd set for myself based on the training I'd been doing. If I'd ridden solely to get the record in London it would have been a different experience. It might have been a tad easier, but the crucial thing for me was to ride to the pace that I thought I was capable of doing on that day. The figure in my head was 55.2km; that was what I was going for. In some ways I didn't even concentrate on Alex's record.

I don't want to sound arrogant but I could have chased the record at any time, even before Alex went for it. I could have come out of Paris–Roubaix and gone after Rohan Dennis's record three days later if I'd had no option. But I didn't want to just get the record. If I was going to do it once – as is probably the case – I wanted to go as far as I possibly could.

Halfway. Thirty minutes on the clock. A huge, uplifting surge of morale. An immense sigh of relief. In half an hour I'll be finished; in a couple of hours I'll be in the bar and it will all be over. Half an hour, such a big thing: I've had to be so controlled in that first 30 minutes, really stick to my schedule, then it quickly starts catching up with me; this is a good mental lift for me because 30 minutes in is when I can start fighting the effort and biting back.

So far, it's been easy – not easy like when you are riding down to the shops on your bike, but well within what I can manage. But while it's comfortable the danger is that I go too hard. It's not hurting, I don't want it to hurt, it's a niggly, pinching pace. Making a conscious effort to rein yourself back is never easy.

After those early, relatively comfortable minutes, a change gradually comes upon me. I start to focus more, stop thinking about all the little things. It's like riding on the turbo trainer while watching a film. You start riding hard, it's fine for a while, and then it starts digging in a bit; you start not watching the film for a few minutes at a time because you are concentrating on riding the bike because it's getting hard. That's intensified the further you get into the record.

The effort started biting a little after 20 minutes and has grown since then, but hitting the half-hour means that I've broken the back of it. Still, I need to keep my spirits up. In 10 minutes I'll see 20 minutes to go – how's that going to feel? I'm over the hump. From now on, it's just a matter of counting down the clock, with the end getting closer and closer.

1 2 3 4 5 6 7 8 9 10 11 12 13 14 15 16 17 18 19 20 21 22 23 24 25 26 27

54.90
54.85
54.82
54.77
54.77
54.71
54.77
54.68
54.72
54.84
54.71
54.63
54.84
54.65
54.63
54.97
54.97
54.62
54.73
54.89
55.14
54.99
55.13
54.94
54.92
54.02
49.81 (km/h for all laps)

30 minutes SPEED PER KILOMETRE

28 29 30 31 32 33 34 35 36 37 38 39 40 41 42 43 44 45 46 47 48 49 50 51 52 53 54

54.87

54.72

54.56 54.61
        54.66
54.53 54.59
54.61
54.61
54.66
54.66
54.65
54.66

54.33

54.47
54.50

54.35

54.19 54.42
54.35

54.18
54.10
54.13
54.18
54.34
54.13

53.99
54.13

Mexico City, 19 January 1984: 50.808km

Mexico City, 23 January 1984: 51.151km

Sea-level Hour, 1986: 48.543km

Sea-level Hour, 1986: 49.801km

Indoor Hour, 1987: 48.637km

Indoor Hour, 1988: 50.644km

Mexico City, on Obree bars,

January 1994: 51.840km

Francesco Moser was way before my time and I wasn't even aware of his Hour Records when I began racing. I might have seen the odd picture of him on that bike with the big wheel. But the point when I became aware of him was in 1994, when he came back to racing aged 43, and rode the Hour Record in Mexico in Graeme Obree's position. That was ten years after he revolutionised the record by breaking Merckx's distance twice in four days. The key thing was that he began using aerodynamic aids which were revolutionary at the time, but which are standard nowadays: low-profile bike, disc wheels, skinsuit. It was after this that everyone became aware of the difference that aerodynamics could make.

His first record was 50.808km which wasn't that much further than Merckx, considering the bike and the kit he had; in some ways that validates Merckx's record even more. I broke Alex's distance by 1.5km but using a similar bike and kit and position. If you look at Moser's he beat Merckx by 1.3km on a completely different bike, set-up and skinsuit on the same track as Eddy, and the track was sprayed to make it smoother. He went again four days later, and did 51.151km, which most people reckoned was unbeatable until Graeme Obree went for it in 1993.

Moser was too big a unit to shine in the mountains, so the Grand Tours weren't really his thing – apart from one Giro win in 1984, which was a bit controversial because a mountain stage got cancelled so some people felt Laurent Fignon was robbed of the win – but he has a superb record as a Classics rider; those three wins in Paris–Roubaix and two in the Tour of Lombardy speak for themselves. After 1984 he kept on at the Hour – he

did at least one outdoor in Milan, one in Stuttgart using a massive back wheel. He then came out of retirement for his last attempt in 1994, partly in order to celebrate the tenth anniversary of his first Record, but it was also an attempt using Graeme's bars. Publicly he said it was to see what difference they would make but I'm sure deep down he wanted to beat Graeme and the others. Even so, knocking out nearly 52km at the age of 43 is quite something.

Vigorelli velodrome, Milan, 7 November 1942: 45.798km

Fausto Coppi is one of those names with a massive story behind it. He was one of the most stylish bike riders the sport has known, and he was the first man to win the Tour and the Giro in the same year – the magic double that only Anquetil, Merckx, Bernard Hinault, Stephen Roche and Indurain have managed. He was the *campionissimo*, the champion of champions, and his rivalry with Gino Bartali is still the stuff of legend. And every cycling fan knows about the great scandal of his divorce, in the days when it was illegal, and how his mistress appeared from nowhere when he won the world championships at Lugano in 1953.

His Hour is one of cycling's great stories: he set it on the outdoor track in Milan where everyone went for the record in those days, and he did it in the middle of the war, in 1942, when the British were bombing the city. They timed the record for the afternoon, as that was when the Lancasters usually held off for a while, but they still had to keep the tunnels under the grandstands clear so that they could be used as an air-raid shelter if the sirens went off.

Coppi couldn't train on the track, because the army had requisitioned it, and there was no petrol to be had so he couldn't do motor-pace training on the road either. So all he could do was find a straight, level bit of road near his home and ride up and down it at record pace, when the army gave him time off. He didn't have a lot of margin on the day, he really struggled, and it wasn't set in stone even when he'd finished; there was a legal challenge from the Frenchman Maurice Archambaud, who held the record, over the way it was measured. That took five years to settle. But the side of it that always gets to you is that not long after the record, Coppi went off with his unit to fight in North Africa and ended up in a prisoner-of-war camp. It's truly the stuff that legends are made of.

⊙ 'Centimetre by centimetre, I managed to catch up with the demonic clock. I could not see the figures on the blackboard. I only knew that I could not fall behind the clock any more . . . My brain knew only the order of the clock: faster, faster, faster!' ⊙ **Fausto Coppi**

Fausto Coppi won the Giro d'Italia five times and the Tour de France twice, as well as holding the Hour Record. He died tragically young at the age of 40

37 minutes

PERMISSION TO HURT

've spoken in the past about getting to my open road. That's the point in an event where your way is clear, the preliminaries are over, there's no real complexity left and it's just down to you. It can be after the first real sort-out in a one-day road race or when you've got through the tricky first week of a Grand Tour, or when the opening part of a time trial is out of the way. Then, all you have to do is turn on the taps and let your body do the rest. In the Hour, you get to your open road in the second half. That's when you can start grimacing and fighting.

Previous page: *My bike, tailor-made by Pinarello and Jaguar. Pinarello also made the bike that Miguel Indurain used for his Hour Record in 1994*

After 30 minutes, you don't have to hold back any more; all you need to think about is how to get through the rest – the tough bit. That's how you manage the Hour; you stay in that controlled state for the first half-hour, then you get to your open road and you fight. When you start fighting, you're not actually going to go much faster but you're working to overcome the messages from your body which is telling you to back off. And time goes differently in each phase – when you are in that first half, the minutes tick by quite quickly, but as it gets more and more intense, time starts going a lot slower, each minute seems to last for ever. The shift happens suddenly once you're past halfway.

The Hour is a big mental battle. You can't afford to start thinking after 20 minutes, 'Bloody hell this is painful' – when there are still 40 minutes to go – so you play games, persuade yourself, 'No, no, it's not hurting yet, I can do half an hour no problem, we've done that in training loads of times'. You have to kid yourself that you're in control of everything. Get 30 minutes under your belt and you can change the way you think. Once you're able to acknowledge it's hurting, then you can start fighting it, admitting, 'It's the hardest thing I've ever done'. Once you get past halfway you've got permission to hurt.

Two of the most important men
in my career. Sir Dave Brailsford
(left), principal of Team Sky, and
Shane Sutton, who is head of rider
performance for the British cycling
team, and who has been my coach
on and off throughout my time on
the bike

The first question when it came to planning the Hour was: who was going to oversee the training? The natural choice was Shane Sutton, who has been a mentor to me since 2002 and was a key member of the back-up team who helped me win the Tour in 2012. I could have asked him, but he's the Great Britain cycling team's performance director now and has pretty much pulled back from doing any front-line training. As I had gone back to riding the track with the team pursuit squad, and as Heiko Salzwedel is their coach, the obvious thing was to ask him to look after that side for me.

I'd worked briefly with Heiko back in 2001 when he was at British Cycling for the first time, and I'd kept in touch with him ever since; he came back for a couple of years after the Beijing Olympics but I didn't see much of him because I was away from the track programme at that point. He's from East Germany; his first Olympic gold medal dates back to Seoul in 1988 when he coached the East German team pursuit squad that beat the Russians. He's had spells in Australia, and with the Russian national team; he's an old-school trainer who reminds me of Jürgen Grobler, who coached Steve Redgrave and Matthew Pinsent to their Olympic medals.

Heiko is very Eastern bloc in his approach: this is what we do, we do seven hours on the bike, we go everywhere as a team. He's enjoyed success pretty much throughout his career, not necessarily always winning but at the very least making smaller cycling nations like Denmark and Switzerland go faster. His teams make gains very rapidly once he takes over. There was quite a turnaround this season when he took over as the GB men's endurance coach and the team pursuiters went from eighth in the world championships to second in the space of 12 months.

The key to this success is that Heiko has 30 years' experience in looking at any given event and taking it apart. Heiko's experience makes him completely different from someone like Tim Kerrison, the physiologist at Team Sky, who did all the groundwork when I won the Tour and took the Olympic time trial in 2012. Leading up to the Tour, it was Tim who worked out all the figures I needed to hit in training to compete in the mountains, and who came up with left-field ideas like training at altitude to replicate the highest climbs. Tim is all about numbers and physiology, and his strength is partly due to coming from a non-cycling background, which means that he can take a completely fresh look at something that appears quite familiar if you've been in the sport for years.

Heiko was the day-to-day coaching presence while Tim had more of an overview, in the same way that when I built up to the Tour Tim did the planning and Shane dealt with the details of each day. Tim and I had a discussion about the Hour on the Team Sky bus at Paris–Nice in March; he worked out how many calories I'd consume in an hour, and the most effective ways to train. Physiologically, the Hour is quite simple – it's just riding

The plan was for me to wear a celebratory jersey with the record-breaking distance on. So Rapha had some designers there ready to stitch on the numbers as soon my Hour was up

consistently at threshold as you would in a time trial – but you can't simply replicate how you would train for a time trial on the road, because everything you do on the track is so intense.

When we were training for the Tour we'd do five- or six-hour rides – you'd hit the last climb up to the hotel in Tenerife and go for 30 minutes at threshold to simulate a Tour stage. But if you rode that far then came on to the track and tried to ride at threshold for half an hour, you wouldn't be able to do it – the intensity, the cadence, the control you have to have on each banking is completely different. So everything we did in training on the track was a balancing act between working hard enough to gain some benefit and making sure I was never too fatigued from any one session to do it again the next day.

The benefit of having someone with Heiko's track experience alongside me showed. Some days we had to abandon training because I was tired, or I'd roll into

the velodrome planning to do a 15km effort and bail out after five kilometres because training on the track is so unforgiving that if you aren't on the money you might as well be resting. On the road you can slog it out up a climb by concentrating on each hairpin; the road might go downhill a bit and give you a breather, or five minutes will go past quicker because you start looking down into the valley. But on the track when you come past your coach for the first time and you see a lap board saying 80 laps to go, you know you will get no breaks in rhythm and there will be nothing to change how you feel. It isn't until you start doing your effort that you find out quite how strong you actually are.

That was where we had to play it carefully with Tim. He's very numbers oriented, and because he hasn't raced on the track it's hard to explain how it feels. We ended up picking and choosing from the programme that he suggested. It would change almost daily depending on my level of fatigue. Shane's experience was useful – he'd come to the track and warn me about doing a session if he felt it was too much. Heiko's got those decades of experience as well, so he'd adapt a lot of the suggestions from Tim. Rather than a three-hour road ride before the track session we might go to the track first, and then I'd ride home, so I'd have the quality training in the bag before the road ride. There wasn't actually much information to be found on how you train for the Hour. It was a learning experience for all of us; the plan wasn't set in stone from day one. But what we have now

is quite a lot of information about what worked and what didn't work for if I ever wanted to do it again.

I had two races in the UK to do before I got to the Hour, and very different ones at that. At the start of May I rode the Tour de Yorkshire, a three-day stage race which is now run in the county as part of the legacy of the 2014 Tour de France Grand Départ. It was a high-profile event that would be the first major race for my new squad, Team Wiggins, so I wanted to take part, and it also fitted in well as preparation for the track because it was a good way of getting in the volume of work, the hours of intensity you get from road racing. Plus it was organised by ASO, who run the Tour de France, and they would definitely accept the team if I rode as well. Two days after the Tour de Yorkshire I did 30 minutes at 55km/h pace in Manchester and it felt easy; we were supposed to have another session the next day but we said, 'Just leave that, go out on the road.'

I had another little objective midway through the build-up when I went for the ten-mile competition record, which, funnily enough, is also held by Alex Dowsett. It fitted the programme, and I'd always wanted to do a '10' as world time trial champion, to show the rainbow jersey on British roads. Time trialling is where I started out – it's all very low-key, it's on open roads, you swap your number afterwards for a cup of tea in the village hall – and it felt like I was giving a bit back to the sport, helping make the event and time trialling more high profile. This one was on a flat, fast course near Hull, but it was a windy day – they put the start back by 45 minutes while a lamp post that had blown over was sorted out – and I missed out on Alex's record by 39sec. There were people lined up on the roadsides, people standing on the bridges to watch. It gave a lot of club cyclists the chance to say they'd raced with a Tour winner; I remember almost catching the guy who'd started five minutes in front of me. He was still a few metres ahead on the line, and he let out a massive roar as he got there in front of me because he'd managed to hold me off. That sort of thing is what sport is all about.

Alongside Heiko and Shane, I had help from Deborah Sides, the performance analyst at British Cycling, who compiled all the graphs at the end of each session. I'd do a training session at the track, get home, and later on I'd get an email with all the data from that day: average power for each effort within the session, average speed, average lap time, kilometre splits, and so on.

In the run-up to the record, I had a small team of people around me. Pete Smith was one; he's a *soigneur* – a big tall guy with grey hair who looks a bit like George Clooney – who has been helping me out since I was eighteen, when he was working for the Great Britain team at the road world championships at Valkenberg in 1998 and I was riding for the junior team. Pete has been around the block with Team Sky – and the American national women's team among others – and now he's with us at Team Wiggins.

David Dunne was my nutritionist – he works at Harlequins Rugby Club, and also at

⊙ 'Once you're able to acknowledge it's hurting, then you can start fighting it, admitting, "It's the hardest thing I've ever done." Once you get past halfway you've got permission to hurt.' ⊙

Carsten Jeppesen and Dimitris
Katsanis were the brains behind
the bike and all the bits of kit

Team Wiggins – so he was in the hotel cooking food for me all week. His younger brother is the golfer Paul Dunne, who in July 2015 became the first amateur since 1927 to be leading the Open after the third round.

I also had the services of Matt Rabin who was the chiropractor at Garmin; I've known him since even before my season racing for them in 2009. He works out of London and it just so happens we went to school together at St Augustine's in Kilburn. He was in the year above me and was expelled; he was a bit wild like most of the kids at that school at the time, but ended up turning his life around. I met him years later in cycling and I can still remember us both doing a double take when we recognised each other.

Carsten Jeppesen and Dimitris Katsanis were the brains behind the bike and all the bits of kit. Carsten has been at Team Sky since Dave Brailsford and Shane Sutton began putting the team together in the spring of 2009, and before that he was with Bjarne Riis at CSC for eight years. He's the Head of Technical Operations and Commercial at Team Sky now, and that means his job is to make sure the riders have the best of everything to work with. So he project-managed the equipment side – he was in charge of getting the bike ready, deciding what wheels we'd be using, and getting chainrings cut because there are no manufacturers who make chainrings as large as 62 teeth, so you have to get them cut specially, and you need a whole selection to enable you to tweak the gearing by switching from, say, a 62 to a 61. Biomechanically, the bigger the chainring you use, the easier it rolls once you've got going, so that's why we went so much larger than the usual track chainring, which would be 51 or 52; on the day we opted for 58x14.

Dimitris was our aerodynamics guru, which is the role he played for years at British Cycling. He was a world-class sprinter for Greece before starting his own manufacturing company to make carbon-fibre parts, and then he became one of Chris Boardman's 'secret squirrels' in the run-up to Beijing; they were the small group who put together the UK Sports Institute carbon-fibre bike that became standard issue for the GB track team. In 2013 he changed direction, and went to work for the UCI as a consultant on equipment, to try and sort out their rules on what could and could not be used; shortly before my Hour attempt, he was hired by Pinarello, the bike makers.

I trained on the UKSI bike that's familiar to anyone who has seen GB at the Olympics; the actual bike turned up a couple of weeks before the event. It was a track version of Pinarello's Bolide – the name comes from the Greek word *bolis*, meaning 'missile' – which is the smoothed-out carbon-fibre machine that Team Sky use and which I rode to win the time trial Worlds in Ponferrada at the end of 2014. It was modified in certain areas, stiffened up by being made one-piece rather than the usual two that are bonded together; Pinarello had to narrow the back end to take track hubs, and made special front forks so that the blades sat closer to the front-wheel surface, making the air flow outside them. And they worked on the fork crown – which could be made tighter because there is

◉ 'The handlebars were the most 'out there' thing, a piece of kit that people hadn't seen before . . . Mine were a one-piece unit, stem and bars together — with the stem profiled back into the frame of the bike — and they were laser-cut in titanium, so I could get precisely the grip I wanted.' ◉

no front brake – and the front dropouts, which were given an aero profile as well.

There are quite a lot of restrictions nowadays on kit, particularly on the track, so there isn't a lot you can work on outside of the standard geometry on your bike; you can't use fancy bits you can buy off the internet and you're not allowed overshoes any more. The wheels were standard discs, the pedals were my usual Speedplay, the aerodynamic helmet was actually the one I won the Olympic time trial with, but sprayed gold. The skinsuit was just standard issue made by Rapha – a good tight fit.

The handlebars were the most 'out there' thing, a piece of kit that people hadn't seen before. They've always been something Hour riders have concentrated on – everyone knows that Graeme Obree made his own, but so did Tony Rominger and so did Chris; he got bike builder Terry Dolan to make them. Mine were a one-piece unit, stem and bars together – with the stem profiled back into the frame of the bike – and they were laser-cut in titanium, so I could get precisely the grip I wanted. No one actually designed them – they were made using pictures of my time-trial positions in the past, looking at where I hold the bars and how I hold them. The technique is actually known as additive layer manufacturing; they were made at the University of Sheffield where they do a 3D scan of your arm position and cut the bar around it, to the precise length of your arms. I tend to grip my hands round the end so I got two pieces of plasticine a week before, and moulded them into what I wanted to hold on to for an hour, what I would be most comfortable with; from those they made two plastic grips for the ends of the bars – like the gear stick in a car. Contrary to what was claimed after the record, anyone can buy their own – Pinarello offer the service through one of their brands, MOST.

I changed my position quite a bit from my usual time-trial style – we did quite a bit of testing at the Manchester Velodrome and I ended up being lower at the front end. It wasn't very sophisticated – we never went near a wind tunnel – it was literally a matter of taking the spacers down at the front and seeing what happened. I'd change the position, ride at a certain speed for three laps, 16.2sec or whatever, and see what power it took. Then we would compare the wattage I needed for different set-ups. We brought the power required to go at Hour speed down by about 30 watts, simply by tweaking the position. There were other little things such as asking, 'Why do you need this great big flat handlebar?' You're only on the outside of the bar for eight seconds at the start as you pull away, and it makes no difference to how quickly you go, because you are trying to get out of the gate so steadily. So we chopped it down, made it smaller. It's all frontal area, and every little helps with aerodynamics.

Alongside Dimitris was Ernie Feargrave, the mechanic who is a bit of an institution at British Cycling. He's been there since I was a junior. He's the best mechanic I've worked with on the track – he's so passionate about it, knows everything about it, and just lives for his job. He worked on Chris's record with him in 1996, and calls him Billy

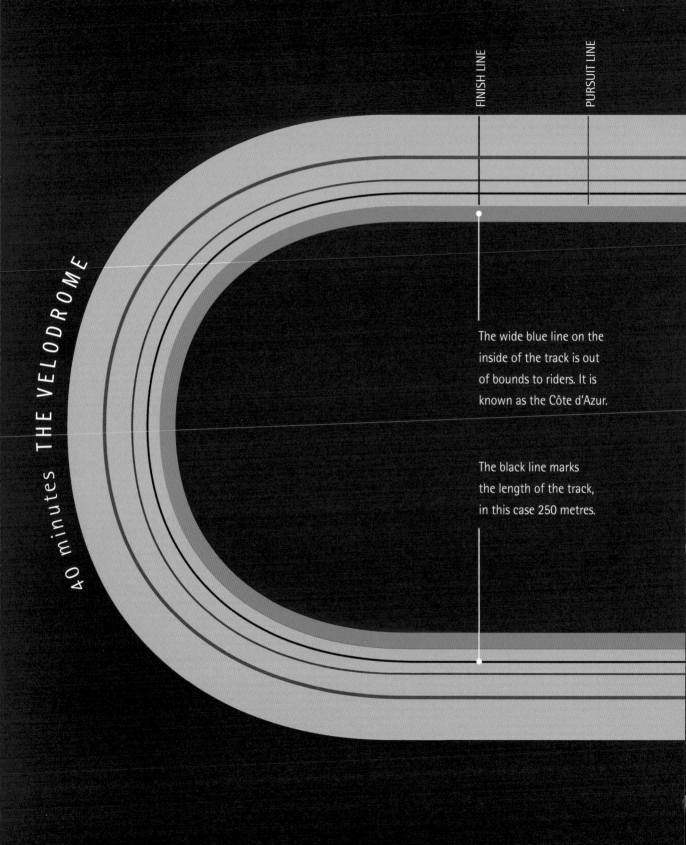

FINISH LINE

PURSUIT LINE

The wide blue line on the inside of the track is out of bounds to riders. It is known as the Côte d'Azur.

The black line marks the length of the track, in this case 250 metres.

RED SPRINTER'S LINE: The area between the red and black lines is the optimum racing line

In Madison races the secondary team rider 'rests' here until his partner brings him into action

Spectators: 6,000

Length of track: 250 metres

Length of Siberian Pine Per Lap: 56 kilometres

Nails Per Lap: 350,000

12 Degrees banking
on the straights

45 Degrees
highest banking
on the turns

BLUE STAYER'S LINE: This outer line serves in stayer races as a separation line.

after Billy Whizz, the cartoon character in the *Beano*. Ernie was in charge of putting the bike together; he'd work into the small hours gluing in bearings and making sure it was immaculate. He wouldn't let anyone else touch it.

The support of my family was also vital – my wife, Cath, and our children, Ben and Bella. As the kids get older my relationship with them seems to change daily. It takes me back to my own childhood and how different it was. I never really had a dad so watching Ben growing up and seeing how a father-and-son relationship develops is a new thing, even just taking him out on the bike for an hour or whatever. He's full on with his cycling at ten years old. He says he has two heroes – Peter Sagan and me. It's funny because I'm his dad and his hero at the same time so he distinguishes between Bradley Wiggins the cyclist when, for example, he watches the Hour Record, and then there is me, his dad. Sometimes they blend into the same person, like when we go out on our bikes together. That means a lot because I never had that and he just loves cycling.

Cath has been there through everything I've done since day one. She said they were happy not to stay with me before the Hour if it might affect my riding, but I wanted them around me, so, for example, I saw them at breakfast that morning. I like the feeling of normality before I go into action. I didn't want to be shut off, because it's as much their day as it is mine – before I left for the track I made sure we got a photograph of the two of us outside the hotel. I feel guilty that I've sacrificed so much family time over the years but then again we've lived some of my most successful moments together – the Tour win, when they were with me and the kids rode down the Champs-Elysées, the Olympics, and now this. I couldn't do any of it without their support and backing. In some ways, I resent what I've achieved, because looking back at those years I don't think I was always a very nice person – so much goes into winning the Tour de France, it's a whole lifestyle. You have to be self-centred. But they could understand why I was doing it, and knew that it didn't reflect who I am underneath.

Watching the kids grow up has helped give me perspective in recent years because they are so much more important than the Hour Record, the Tour de France or whatever I'm training for. That gives me a certain calmness when I'm doing these things, because the racing is no longer the be-all and end-all. Ten years ago, and when I was a kid, it felt like a matter of life or death. I'll never forget being on the start line at the individual pursuit at the Athens Olympics in 2004, and thinking, 'What I am I going to do if I don't beat Brad McGee? How is life going to go on?' Having a family helps you deal with these big occasions. They are a motivation for you to go out and train for the key races in the first place, because you are doing it for someone else, but then when you get to the actual event, knowing your family are there to watch has a reassuring effect, because that reminds you that life will go on after it no matter how you do. Finding that perspective gets easier as you get older and your thought processes get more rational and logical.

I'm through 35 minutes. My mind has started wandering. 'Shit, this is hard', 'Right, are we going to do this?' – that kind of train of thought. I'm constantly telling myself, every lap it seems, things like 'In three more minutes you've got 20 minutes to go, just a couple more minutes'. At 37 minutes I'm thinking, 'Ten minutes from now you're going to have 13 minutes to go – you're nearly there.' So although I've got 23 minutes to go I'm cutting it in half to make it seem manageable, giving myself those little targets all the time. I need to pick myself up.

It was Ritter's record from 1968 that Eddy Merckx broke in 1972, but the Dane's real claim to fame is through *The Impossible Hour*, the film that Jørgen Leth made about him and his obsession with the record. Leth's films about cycling – *Stars and Watercarriers, A Sunday in Hell* – are must-sees for cycling fans. Like the others, this is pure seventies nostalgia: Ritter's massive sideburns, the thin handlebar tape on his Benotto bike, the old-school Campagnolo bits, woolly tights and jerseys, plus the scene where he is training behind a motorbike driven by a guy with no crash-helmet, hair blowing in the wind.

Ritter was a bit like Chris Boardman, a time-trial specialist who turned to the Hour as the natural thing to do next. His position on the bike was fabulous, and so was his style when he rode – no movement in the shoulders, flat back. He was capable of beating Merckx on occasion, but mainly he was in the same boat as all the pros in the early 1970s, constantly frustrated by Merckx's dominance. And in 1968 he became the first to take the record at altitude in Mexico, a fashion that lasted until the 1990s.

What strikes you about the film is firstly that it's beautifully shot; but more than that, it's about failure. Ritter is determined to get his record back from Merckx, and he keeps going for it. He manages to beat his record from 1968, twice in the space of a week, but he can't get Eddy's distance. He's not far off – the second one is 48.879km to Eddy's 49.431 – but that's the point about this record: there is nothing to be gained by coming second.

Vélodrome de Bordeaux Lac, 23 July 1993: 52.270km
Manchester Velodrome, 6 September 1996: 56.375km
Athlete's Hour, Manchester, 27 October 2000: 49.441km

It was Chris who really began to change cycling when he came along in 1994; I still remember him coming down the boulevard in Lille to win the prologue time trial in that year's Tour de France, with only his back visible in the television coverage from behind because he was so aerodynamic on the bike. In those days people thought less about aerodynamics when it came to time trialling, it was more a matter of immense human effort, which was how Miguel Indurain rode every time trial. But Chris put 15–20sec into the likes of Tony Rominger and Indurain in just over seven kilometres.

I was watching the prologue in 2015, with Chris commentating for ITV, and I realised it was 20 years since he had crashed out in Saint-Brieuc in the 1995 Tour prologue and Jacky Durand ended up winning the stage. It seemed like yesterday to me. Back then I was 15 years old and glued to it; it seemed so space-age and modern to me.

Chris's achievements were crucial to my career. Right through my teenage years he was Britain's best cyclist. I watched him winning gold at the Barcelona Olympics in 1992 when I was 12 and was inspired; then there was his Hour Record in 1993, then Lille the next year when he won the Tour prologue, the 1995 Tour when he crashed, and in 1996 the Hour again. He was different – he brought out a whole new side to cycling with the Lotus bike, the aerodynamic carbon-fibre machine that everyone talked about in 1992. He wasn't a one-trick pony either; he could finish second overall to Pavel Tonkov in the Tour de Romandie, or second to Miguel Indurain in the Dauphiné – good results just behind two Grand Tour winners.

Then he retired and returned to British Cycling and helped me with the pursuit project in the run-up to Athens. He's always been a sounding board for me and when it came to taking on the Hour he was the first person I was going to talk to. Initially we spoke about

Chris Boardman tackling the Athlete's Hour. His attempt bested Merckx, but using similar equipment to Merckx's 1972 record. His coach Peter Keen is keeping him posted on his progress

⊙ 'It is amazing how long an hour can last. I have never been in this much pain in my life . . . I had no idea if I would pass the distance. I just wanted it to end. It was most unpleasant for a couple of minutes, which felt like a couple of years.' ⊙ **Chris Boardman**

it at a training camp in Majorca in January 2015 – what's it like to do the Hour? What do you think? And he asked me a load of questions: where are you going to do it? Who's going to be the project manager? From that chat he said it looked like I had most of it covered, and I had a background in track racing and time trialling like he did, so it shouldn't be too difficult. He's been a mainstay throughout my time in cycling.

Boardman's gold-medal-winning performance at the Barcelona Olympics in 1992 was one of my main inspirations as a young cyclist

47 minutes

INTO THE UNKNOWN

No one can know what the last 15 minutes of an Hour Record attempt is going to be like until they get there for the first time. I've been dealing with that uncertainty all through the winter and spring. I've tried to rationalise it by comparing it to other tough days I've had on the bike. I've told myself that I should be fine after feeling good in the dress rehearsal, but I have no real idea.

Over page: *Winning the time trial at Chartres that secured overall victory in the 2012 Tour de France*

Most importantly, I've got to stay relaxed and keep focusing on my form and getting that banking/straight squeeze/ease rhythm just right. I used to row a little bit 10 or 15 years ago – in the off-season, I would nip down to Henley now and then with a friend of mine in London on a Saturday morning, just for something else to do other than riding the bike. Riding on the track under pressure, real pressure, is very similar to rowing double sculls – there is a lot of technique involved. When you watch it on the telly the rowers make it look easy, but when they start to get fatigued in the final of something like the Olympics it's not like being on a rowing machine where it's just a matter of brute force, they've still got to keep the boat moving in a stable way.

During the Hour the last few minutes are about keeping the inertia going with the effort you're putting into it. You can't begin stabbing at the pedals, because every time you lose that smoothness you end up slowing down a little bit and then you have to pick up the pace again. You need to be as consistent with your speed as you can be. You have to keep your mind focused in spite of the suffering – it's not just about grinding it out like you see people do up the climbs where they are swaying all over their bike, forcing it, doing everything to keep that effort going. Riding the track well is about keeping your form: that's what I've got to do now.

I've got to blank everything out apart from keeping

'I left home on 1 July 2012 relatively unknown in the eyes of the general public, and I came home three weeks later as the first Briton to win the Tour to a country that had gone cycling mad.'

those pedals rolling smoothly, not chucking my weight at them. But it's like a boxing ring in here, the deafening noise, the heat, the dryness in my throat. Apart from the din of the crowd, the only sound is the echoing roar of the disc wheels every eight seconds as I go through each banking, like someone swooshing out a first service at 100mph at Wimbledon. There is the occasional really huge roar from the spectators – that must be when the screen shows how far I'm up on Alex Dowsett – every five kilometres, so maybe every six minutes.

The last 15 minutes of any time trial is never a good place to be, but it's always been the same: Ponferrada, Hampton Court, Chartres. But how's it going to be with the Hour? There is only one way to find out and that's what I'm going to do now, whether I like it or not.

I remember watching a film called *Overcoming*, which was about CSC and Bjarne Riis, who said something that's stuck with me for ten years: his philosophy was 'You never know how hard you can tighten something until it breaks'. Whether you are training, overtraining, or trying to get to your perfect race weight, you never know how far to push yourself until you actually break down. That's always stayed with me, no matter what I've done. I like that idea. It's true of time trialling, pursuiting or riding the Tour de France – how far do you push the envelope? And I guess you can apply it to the Hour Record as well, because just the same as in any timed event, you only have to go a little bit over the edge before you break down altogether.

The challenges I've set myself throughout my career have been quite big, quite bold. There had to be a huge risk of failure, because that is what would make me think it was worth pushing myself. I've always felt that the bar had to be set really high, to make sure that I truly had to respect what I was doing. That's probably why I've rarely gone back and repeated the things I've done, apart from trying to defend my Olympic individual pursuit title in Beijing in 2008. I like doing different things in cycling and I like the versatility that calls for: pursuits – individual and team – madison, Paris–Nice, the Tour de France, world time trial championships, Paris–Roubaix, the Hour Record, and finally back to the team pursuit.

I like the freshness of starting something different, the challenge of training for disciplines which make very different demands on you – so in the run-up to the Rio Olympics in 2016 I'm training to be faster and stronger for an intense 3min 50sec on the bike rather than to last the three weeks of a Grand Tour. I like that contrast, and I like the idea of changing my body shape – for Rio, it's a matter of putting on muscle and becoming more powerful. I've always been fascinated by how far you can push the body one way or the other, whether it's trying to get as lean as possible for climbing or trying

Left: *Ringing the bell to open the 2012 Olympic Games in London.* Right: *On my way to winning Olympic gold to cap a crazy month-long period*

to build muscle mass without panicking about weight. I like the fact that with the nutrition side, it's a measurable effort for a definite outcome: if you do this, you will achieve that. When I was building up for the Tour, I liked the extremity of not eating and then trying to do seven hours on the bike to drop as much weight as I could. That was as much a part of the game as training and racing – it's about finding out what you can make your body do.

It's been 15 years since I sat in the track centre at the Manchester Velodrome with Graeme Obree, fresh from getting my bronze medal in the Sydney Olympics, watching Chris Boardman finish his career with his Athlete's Hour. I still feel like the same person inside, although I was 20 then and a lot has happened since. I know I'm now a lot wiser, more comfortable in my own skin. I've experienced some pretty extreme events as a bike racer and they have had a big effect, above all when

I won the Tour and then the Olympic time trial in the space of ten days in 2012. That feels like it was the pinnacle of my career; there is a before and an after. I guess I was building up to that from when I was a kid all the way through everything I did on the track and beyond.

I left home on 1 July 2012 relatively unknown in the eyes of the general public, and I came home three weeks later as the first Briton to win the Tour to a country that had gone cycling mad. The events of those couple of weeks will never be repeated, at least not during my career. I said it at the time in Hampton Court, when I won Olympic gold, that this would never, ever get any better for me. I remember Dave Brailsford saying, 'Don't say that, you want to keep your options open,' but I was certain: 'Dave, it's not going to happen again.'

It was a unique time, a very special time for me and for cycling in Britain. Look back at the end of the 2012 Tour and ask yourself this: will it ever happen again that the winner of the Tour will be leading out the world champion on the Champs- Elysées, who will win the stage? Because that's exactly what happened when I led Mark Cavendish out in 2012. In the foreseeable future there will be riders who win the Tour de France who are capable of doing the lead-out on the Champs-Elysées for a rider who could win it, but we'd need

*Ponferrada, 2014: Walking to the
podium as winner of the time trial
at the UCI world championships*

a sprinter to be a world champion again, so the chances of it happening are pretty slim. But could it happen that both of them, one in the yellow jersey, one in the rainbow jersey, are British and riding for a British team? That in itself was a unique, historic moment, not to mention the fact that a week later there was a home Games, in London, with all those gold medals.

I came back to Britain and felt like the most famous man in the country after winning the Tour – and if I wasn't, then I was after I'd rung the bell at the opening ceremony at the Olympic stadium, followed by going on to win that time trial. It changed everything for the kids, for Cath and me, and that was all thrust upon us in four weeks with no warning, because it's not something you can prepare for. For those few weeks it was just crazy. We couldn't go anywhere in London without security. I had been in the bubble of leading the Tour for two weeks, not knowing what was being said back home in the newspapers and on television, with no idea about the hype building before the Olympics. Then I came home from the Tour de France to find all the press outside my house. I couldn't leave in a car to go to the Olympics because of all the media and fans outside, so I got in a helicopter which landed in my back garden and flew to this little landing strip near London to be met by Chris Lillywhite from the GB team before I rode the Olympic road race.

Having to deal with that massive upheaval in my life took until the following June, when it then became clear that I wasn't going to start the 2013 Tour; it was probably the worst period of my life, in a sporting sense, because I didn't know whether I was coming or going or what I was doing next. So much had changed. I couldn't go anywhere without being recognised and that started to impact on everything we were trying to do, whether it was going on holiday, taking the kids for a pizza or whatever.

That experience had an effect on me. I was forced to change, I've come out the other side and I'm stable again; I know how to handle those situations. We trained so hard for all those years to win the Tour de France but there was no rule book we could look at to tell us about afterwards, how our lives were going to be turned upside down. What you discover is that you've achieved this massive thing, but you can't just go on holiday to Pollença like you always used to, and expect everything to be the same. That took a long time to get my head around. I tried to force it, and keep life as normal as possible, but actually I had to realise that things had changed for ever.

Back then, watching Chis Boardman with Graeme Obree, I was such a fan of the sport. I idolised people in it – Chris, one of my childhood heroes, was riding his last race. Fifteen years on, because I've pretty much moved out of the road-racing world now, it's been almost like dying. People start writing your obituary and judging you by what you've achieved, rather than by what you are going to do next. I noticed that when I announced that I would finish with Team Sky at Paris–Roubaix in April 2015. People

Wearing the rainbow stripes of world champion was a huge honour.
Next page: *Exhausted after giving everything I had in my last ever race for Team Sky, Paris–Roubaix in April 2015*

BRADLEY'S PALMARES

1998 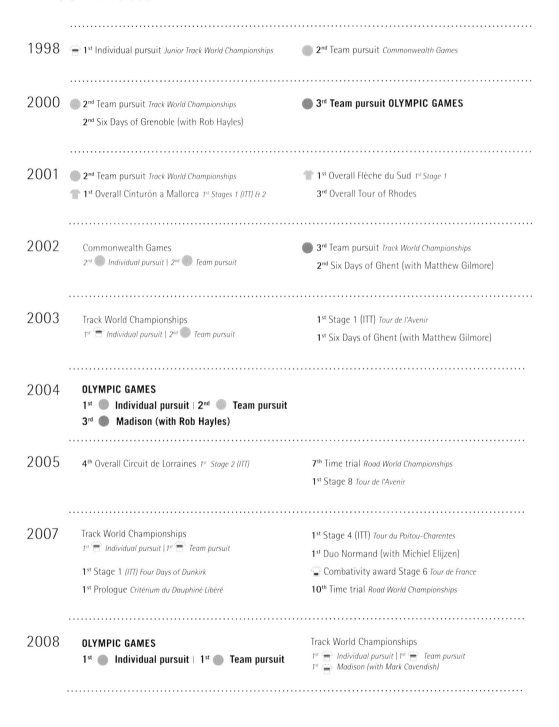 1st Individual pursuit *Junior Track World Championships*   2nd Team pursuit *Commonwealth Games*

2000 2nd Team pursuit *Track World Championships*   **3rd Team pursuit OLYMPIC GAMES**
2nd Six Days of Grenoble (with Rob Hayles)

2001 2nd Team pursuit *Track World Championships*   1st Overall Flèche du Sud *1st Stage 1*
1st Overall Cinturón a Mallorca *1st Stages 1 (ITT) & 2*   3rd Overall Tour of Rhodes

2002 Commonwealth Games   3rd Team pursuit *Track World Championships*
2nd Individual pursuit | *2nd* Team pursuit   2nd Six Days of Ghent (with Matthew Gilmore)

2003 Track World Championships   1st Stage 1 (ITT) *Tour de l'Avenir*
1st Individual pursuit | *2nd* Team pursuit   1st Six Days of Ghent (with Matthew Gilmore)

2004 **OLYMPIC GAMES**
1st Individual pursuit | 2nd Team pursuit
3rd Madison (with Rob Hayles)

2005 4th Overall Circuit de Lorraines *1st Stage 2 (ITT)*   7th Time trial *Road World Championships*
1st Stage 8 *Tour de l'Avenir*

2007 Track World Championships   1st Stage 4 (ITT) *Tour du Poitou-Charentes*
1st Individual pursuit | *1st* Team pursuit   1st Duo Normand (with Michiel Elijzen)
1st Stage 1 *(ITT) Four Days of Dunkirk*   Combativity award Stage 6 *Tour de France*
1st Prologue *Critérium du Dauphiné Libéré*   10th Time trial *Road World Championships*

2008 **OLYMPIC GAMES**   Track World Championships
1st Individual pursuit | 1st Team pursuit   *1st* Individual pursuit | *1st* Team pursuit
1st Madison (with Mark Cavendish)

2009   1st National Time Trial Championships

1st Overall Herald Sun Tour *1st Stage 5 (ITT)*

1st Stage 1 (TTT) *Tour of Qatar*

1st Stage 3b (ITT) *Three Days of De Panne*

1st Beaumont Trophy

3rd Overall TOUR DE FRANCE

2010   1st National Time Trial Championships

1st Stage 1 (TTT) Tour of Qatar

1st Stage 1 (ITT) *Giro d'Italia*

Held Pink Jersey for Stage 2

3rd Overall Vuelta a Murcia

2011   1st National Time Trial Championships

1st Overall Critérium du Dauphiné

1st Stage 4 (ITT) *Bayern-Rundfahrt*

2nd Time trial *Road World Championships*

3rd Overall Paris–Nice

3rd Overall VUELTA A ESPAÑA

Held Red Jersey from Stages 11–15

2012   1st **Overall TOUR DE FRANCE**

1st Stages 9 (ITT) & 19 (ITT)

1st Overall Paris–Nice

1st Points classification | 1st Stage 8 (ITT)

1st Overall Tour de Romandie *1st Stages 1 & 5 (ITT)*

1st Overall Critérium du Dauphiné *1st Stage 4 (ITT)*

1st Time trial OLYMPIC GAMES

3rd Overall Volta ao Algarve *1st Stage 5 (ITT)*

2013   1st **Overall TOUR OF BRITAIN** 1st **Stage 3 (ITT)**

1st Stage 7 (ITT) *Tour de Pologne*

1st Stage 2 (TTT) *Giro d'Italia*

2nd Time trial *Road World Championships*

5th Overall Giro del Trentino *1st Stage 1b (TTT)*

5th Overall Volta a Catalunya

2014   1st **Time trial ROAD WORLD CHAMPIONSHIPS**

1st National Time Trial Championships

1st Overall Tour of California *1st Stage 2 (ITT)*

2nd Team pursuit *Commonwealth Games*

3rd Overall Tour of Britain *1st Stage 8a (ITT)*

9th Paris–Roubaix

2015   Revolution Series *Round 1 (Derby)*

1st Team pursuit
1st Madison, (with Mark Cavendish)

3rd Overall Three Days of De Panne *1st Stage 3b (ITT)*

THE HOUR RECORD! (54.526km)

started celebrating what I'd accomplished, writing articles about what I'd done, as if I was retiring. I wasn't: one phase had come to an end, that's all. One particular British magazine had a whole edition on celebrating my legacy, claiming that I was the greatest cyclist Britain had produced – and that's weird because I haven't finished yet, plus I'd never put myself in the same category as someone like Tom Simpson. I find the thought embarrassing. Even though I won the Tour de France, I have never seen myself in that category. It's like when people talk about becoming the 'greatest Olympian – you're going to have the most medals' – I'm just happy to be in there behind Steve Redgrave and Sir Chris Hoy but I'd never see myself in the same class as those guys. I'm content on the fringes and to be in a little club with some of them and it's the same with the Hour Record: I'm happy to be in that list of people who've won the Tour and held the record along with Indurain, Merckx and Rominger. It's great to be in that company but I'd never compare myself to those guys.

When I didn't make the Tour de France team for Team Sky in the summer of 2014 it raised the question: what was I going to do next? It was 18 months out from the Rio Olympics and I was going to have to start thinking seriously about getting on the track if I wanted to have a proper go at bowing out with one final medal in the team pursuit. I like the circular sense of that, with my career beginning with a team pursuit bronze medal at Sydney in 2000. But getting a place in that team pursuit squad won't be easy, because by the time Rio comes I'll be 36. The event is far more about pure speed than the stamina you gain with age; there is no shortage of younger riders who want the same thing and the Great Britain cycling team doesn't dish out places based on what you've achieved in the past.

I didn't think I would be able to juggle riding for Team Sky and being a winner of the Tour de France with preparing for the track. When you go to races with Team Sky they quite rightly expect a certain standard, and if I was going to concentrate on the track, what I could offer them on the road was only going to diminish. On a track training programme focused on power and speed, I was going to start getting dropped on climbs at races like Paris–Nice and then there would be comments like: 'This guy won the Tour, now look at him'. That led me to switch to the one-day Classics for the spring of 2015, because, with my eye on racing on the track in the long term, I was not going to be able to concentrate on riding stage races for the overall classification any more; trying to be lighter for the road would compromise what we were doing on the track so I needed to make a clean break.

The change of direction in 2014 also led to the foundation of Team Wiggins, which is a UCI Continental team that races mainly a British programme, and largely consists of riders who are in contention for the team pursuit. I was sat at home twiddling my thumbs and I thought, 'I'll have my own team next year, sod this'. It's partly about helping some of the next generation of cyclists, passing down the experience I've got to riders who are in the same position that I was back in the late 1990s when I turned pro for Linda McCartney and it lasted a whole two weeks before the team collapsed.

There are some promising young riders in there, like Owain Doull, who did really well in the Tour of Britain in September 2015 and is clearly heading for a career in Europe as a pro once the Rio Olympics are over. For the moment, everything we do with the team is aimed at facilitating what we are doing on the track – the same guys racing together, being around each other on a daily basis whether we are competing on the road or training on the track. It's worked out really well. We have one goal. We aren't trying to conquer the world, not trying to win the Tour de France. It's about winning gold in Rio. Team Wiggins also means we can embrace and celebrate the history of cycling – the kit design is a nod to the past, based on the old GB blue and red.

In 2014 I ended up watching the Tour and bits and pieces of the Giro as a fan and it made me realise that actually I'm glad I'm not doing that now. I don't feel an ounce of regret seeing all the crashes and so on. It seems that the first week in both the Giro and Tour has just become more and more dangerous. I look forward to the Grand Tours now like any other cycling fan; after watching the 2015 Tour I've started to have visions of Team Wiggins being in France in three years' time, not to try to win it, but to try and mix it up, break the rules a little bit. Looking at the race this year, you can't help seeing how serious everyone is now: riders don't come out of their buses until the last minute because the race has become all about the questions people get asked. I actually thought the biggest success story of this year's Tour was MTN-Qhubeka. They took the Tour back 20 years to how it used to be. Daniel Teklehaimanot from Eritrea wearing the King of the Mountains jersey for those few days – I thought that was the biggest result of the race. It was a breath of fresh air for the Tour, just like when the Colombians turned up in the 1980s and surprised everyone by outperforming other, richer, more established teams.

Something has to change because the Tour can't go on being such a hostile environment for the riders. I'd love to break the mould – go there with Team Wiggins and get back to how it used to be: guys sitting on their team car bonnets putting their shoes on, being a bit more accessible to the public, not just there behind tinted glass to win overall at any cost amid all the pressure that goes with that. I would like the team to be racing and having fun. I have visions of being at the Tour with Cav, Tom Boonen and Philippe Gilbert, elder statesmen at the end of their careers – a bit like 7-Eleven at the end of the1980s – going there and trying to win a stage. I like the way Giant-Alpecin do it: they seem to have a good time balanced with being focused when it matters and getting results, so too do Orica-GreenEDGE. To me, that's how cycling used to be, with teams like Motorola, before it all got too serious. In the post-Armstrong era cycling fans need to fall in love with teams and riders again, with the characters. That's what is going

to win people over.

Rio is next on the horizon for me, but even after that I'm not going to stop riding my bike. After riding a madison with Cav at the Revolution meeting in Derby in August 2015 I said to Cath that it had been seven years since I rode a bunched race on the track, and it felt like being 15 again, back at Reading Track League or Herne Hill. I said, 'I'll probably still ride track league at Manchester when I retire', and I wasn't joking. I might end up doing the World Masters or something but I'll probably ride club ten-mile time trials like Sean Yates did; he retired and then did the national '25' a year later. Just because you've won the Tour de France there's no reason why you should retire completely and never come back to race again at a grass-roots level. The point is this: why stop doing something you love and that you've always done?

⊙ 'It's like a boxing ring in here, the deafening noise, the heat, the dryness in my throat. Apart from the din of the crowd, the only sound is the echoing roar of the disc wheels every eight seconds as I go through each banking.' ⊙

Twelve minutes to go. I'm physically moving about on the saddle. Not a lot, just little shifts of position to ease the numbness in my arse. I can feel it getting slowly worse and worse as I keep telling myself, 'Banking, straight, banking, straight, look at Heiko, banking, press a bit, straight'. I try not to allow myself to think, 'This is hurting'. More and more I begin thinking, 'I can't wait for this to be finished, so I can get off the saddle'. Quick body check: feet, I can feel them; shoulders and neck, OK; hands, they are fine, but so they should be, my position has always been relaxed, I'm not pulling on the bars, just resting them there. I'm pushing down through that bloody saddle. It's not the saddle that's the problem – it's a good one, my usual road saddle from Fizik. Everyone gets it: what do you expect when you are sitting on a damned saddle for an hour with those G forces. There's no shying away from it: I'll do 220 laps, that's 440 times through the bankings. More if I can. I wonder how big that G force actually is, all that gravity pushing through my backside every eight seconds. How on earth did Merckx last an hour on that plastic thing he used?

There's no feeling from my stomach downwards. I'm desperate to move to ease the tension in my backside. I'm just hanging on now. I keep telling myself, 'Eleven minutes to go: that's 40 laps, that's not too bad, the last ten will look after themselves. I just want it to be over. I've had enough of this now. There's ten minutes: got there at last, I've just got to hang on for this next ten minutes. But how long are they going to feel like?'

Vélodrome de Bordeaux Lac, 2 September 1994: 53.040km

When I began cycling in the early nineties there weren't many races on the telly, there was no internet or Twitter and the newspaper coverage wasn't that good. To find out what was going on in the sport you had to wait until Thursday when *Cycling Weekly* came out. It seems crazy now, but I had to wait six days before finding out whether Indurain had broken the Hour record or not; I remember he went for it on a Friday – 2 September 1994 – and on the next Thursday I got my 'comic' and the front cover had a picture of Miguel and the figures 53.040. I just thought 'Wow!' Miguel was a hero of my early years: when it came to Tour time, he was the man, winning it five years on the trot from 1991 to 1995, and in two of those years, 1992 and 1993, he did the double by winning the Giro too. He was a big, hulking bloke, with a perfect tan, who would kill off the opposition in the time-trial stages, then control the race in the mountains.

Following Miguel was part of my routine on Thursdays: I used to come out of school during my lunch break, go down to WH Smith on Kilburn High Road and buy *Cycling Weekly*, then take it back into school. It was a really nice thing to do, like buying a record or CD and pulling it out of the sleeve and reading all the notes. It was the same kind of physical thing with getting *Cycling Weekly*. I'd cut the pictures out and stick them on my wall. And back then, with cycling being such a minority pastime, your newsagent would only order in a certain number of magazines. Smith's would only get two copies because there were only two cyclists living near Kilburn High Road; one was for me and one was for a guy called Mick Clark, who ran a company called Sport and Publicity who sponsored me for a while. He came to see the Hour too.

Miguel Indurain is a five-time
winner of Tour de France.
I remember watching him
dominating the Tour when I first
started following the sport.
Over page: Miguel hitting 53.040
on his Pinarello in 1994

We based my training on what Indurain did, after reading that old article from *Cycle Sport*. I did get to talk to Indurain about it, at the Pinarello Gran Fondo, where I had dinner with him. But he doesn't speak any English and we were talking with Fausto Pinarello translating. Miguel was so blasé about it. I asked what training he did, and he said, 'Nothing because I did it a few weeks after the Tour. I just did it to hold the record, I wasn't interested in putting it out of sight. I just wanted to get my name on the list.' He said his training was the Tour and he just dialled in to what pace he needed once he got on the track. I've watched his record on YouTube – his position is terrible. He couldn't get lower on the bike because he found it too painful – but I think in those days they didn't really know about aerodynamics. That was as advanced as it got with that bike, the Pinarello Espada, which wasn't a bad machine at all. They say he averaged 507 watts for the Hour so he just beasted it out for the 60 minutes. With what we know now about aerodynamics and the power Miguel could produce it's frightening to think what he could have done for an Hour if he had sat a little bit better on his bike.

Amateur record: Velodromo Vigorelli, Milan, 30 October 1954: 44.870km
Professional record: Velodromo Vigorelli, Milan, 19 September 1956: 46.394km

What I love about cycling are the links that run through the sport, the things that connect the great riders and the races and the legendary places with each other, which is why I was so pleased when Ercole Baldini sent me a copy of his book after my Hour Record, with a message saying that he had enjoyed watching it, and just wished he had been there, but that he is now too old to travel.

At 82, Baldini is a living legend, one of the few surviving ex-riders who raced with Fausto Coppi – he even won the Baracchi Trophy two-man team time trial with Coppi back in 1957. There are little things that his career had in common with mine: he's one of the few cyclists to have won an Olympic gold medal and a professional world championship gold as well, although both of his came in the road race. That is truly remarkable, as it's so hard to win a major one-day race. Like me, he was a pursuiter – although most of the top pros were back then - who took the Worlds in 1956, the year he won the Games road race in Melbourne. And he has one Grand Tour victory to his name, in his case the Giro in 1958.

Baldini took the Hour twice, in 1954 as an amateur – this was the time when there were separate records for amateurs and pros – and two years later, when he was still an amateur, he took the professional record off none other than Jacques Anquetil, who went on to win the Tour five times. He was the last amateur to beat the pros before Graeme Obree in 1993. He set both his records on the Vigorelli, the legendary velodrome in Milan, which

is still there, although it's not used any more. And to top it all, he's also got one of the great nicknames: the Locomotive of Forlì. All of which helps explain why I'm going to treasure that book and that note.

57 minutes

GET ME OFF MY BIKE

Seven minutes to go. I tell myself, 'Try not to look at the clock for ten laps now.' Two laps later, I can't help it. 'Six minutes. Oh shit.' I'm glancing at that damned screen all the time. I can't get away from it. I can't ignore it. I want to get off the bike. It's not just the actual effort of turning that blasted gear at 105 revs per minute, and thinking, 'Banking, straight, banking, straight,' it's a feeling: 'I need to get off this bloody bike now.' It's horrific, really painful. Then there's the numbness – I've barely got any feeling between my stomach and my thighs. I'm trying to block out the pain in my backside: I want to move around in the saddle but the slightest shift in position makes it worse. My mouth is drying up: how hot is it in here now? It can't still be 28 degrees?

Opposite: Lifting my bike in the air at the end of sixty minutes, just feeling total relief that it's over

I'm in that red zone where you can't go any harder, you're just hanging on to your pace, you're waiting for it to end. I've got to keep my form: avoid hitting those sandbags on the left, keep watching that black line. I know my head is dropping, I can feel my line changing, then I pull it back, each time it's harder. I'm definitely a bit out of it now. I'm keeping the effort going, but the splits tell me I'm going slightly slower all the time; I haven't hit the wall yet, but it's not far away. I'm trying to stop clock-watching but I just can't help looking. How can each minute take so long to pass?

It's the last five minutes; the fatigue distracts me from my pedalling on one banking, so I lose a little bit, come round, see a slower lap split, then pedal harder to make up for it. The drift between the splits seems huge. So I pedal too hard in the straight and recover on the banking, which is completely wrong. This is just about survival. I'm losing it.

Zero on the clock, but I've got 60 seconds to go. The last minute – I'll try and lift the pace like I always do,

but there is nothing left, no response from my legs. Still, I can sense the end: 'It's done now, this is done.' I'm so happy to be finished. The gun goes: relief. Thank God it's over: 54.526km. I know what it's going to be like, as it's the same when you finish any race: you have a picture of what you're going to do, how you're going to celebrate but you end up doing what comes naturally. I've seen it watching Indurain, Rominger and Boardman's Hours on DVD: that visible euphoria that it's over. It's actually done, that Hour is over.

I'm just so pleased that I can move at last, although I have to sit straight back down again, because I've got no strength in my legs. I can't find a comfortable position for my backside even now. After this I'll be getting the drinks in at the bar standing up. I manage a warm-down lap or two, and then I remember the image I've seen watching videos of Indurain's Hour during the week. Miguel never went overboard with celebrations, but he used to do what I call the Indurain punch – a modest push of the fist up into the air. Let's make that gesture, the Indurain salute. Ernie Feargrave catches me as I slow up, and then I roll up the banking on the finishing straight by the rail so I'm elevated above the crowds, then I can get off and hoist the bike in the air. Then I try to walk back down and it hits me: there's nothing left in my legs. They are buckling. I find Cath – there's nothing better than that hug when it's all over – and then I drop to the floor.

JAGUAR
PINARELLO
WIGGINS
WIGGIN
sky
sky
GREAT BRITAIN
CYCLING TEAM

That was when the cycling fan in me came out a little bit. I felt like I'd joined a club and it was even better as I knew Miguel was there too. Afterwards he came up to the trackside; Fausto Pinarello pushed him to the front. He muttered something in Spanish, probably *'Felicidades';* he seemed a little bit overwhelmed. He's such a gentleman, I don't think he wanted to encroach on my moment, but I wanted him to be there. To have someone like him – a five-time Tour winner, one of the all-time greats with Anquetil, Merckx, Coppi and Hinault – present as I rode my Hour was an honour. I've got one of his yellow jerseys and when I found out he was coming to London I asked Cath to bring it so we could get him to sign it.

As it turned out, I didn't get past Rominger's record from 1995, or Chris's ultimate distance of 56.375km, but I did manage to go beyond Boardman's first record, both of Moser's, Indurain's and Obree's. It's a really respectable distance, 54.526km. It was not as far as I wanted to go but I couldn't have done any more in the conditions. It's right up there; on another day with lower air pressure I probably could get close to Rominger or go further. It would be nice to go as far as he did.

Once the record is in the books, it's there to be beaten. I think the record is breakable at the moment but anyone trying for it will have a job. I was lucky that I had a lot of margin for error for my attempt, and that weighed heavily on my decision to go for it. I put pressure on myself, but it was not by comparing myself to Alex Dowsett, rather in trying to get near Rominger, and ultimately Boardman. What I did manage to do was to raise the bar a fair bit with the new record. I'm sure that distance will deter people and make them think twice about going for it. It's the first big marker since the UCI relaunched the Hour and for the sake of the record – its prestige, its profile – it would be nice if someone attacks my distance within a year or so, even if they fail. The period between Jens's record and mine was a great time, one of those spells when people just go for it again and again, and we have to thank Jens for that for putting himself up there the day after his forty-first birthday.

*The last thing I wanted to do was
get back on a bike again, but I
wanted to do a lap of honour to
thank the fans for coming along*

Personally, I'd love to see Fabian Cancellara and Tony Martin put their hats in the ring even if they haven't got a track pedigree. I think Alex Dowsett will have a good look at what I did, and consider his options; I know he will go away and do his homework – he's a rider who pays attention to details like the aerodynamics, the same as I do. At his age, he's got another eight years or so to think about it, but Fabian and Tony are running out of time. It would be good to see more Grand Tour riders do it – Tom Dumoulin could be next if he gets it right. If he goes to Mexico or gets the right conditions at sea level he can get the record in the next ten years. As for me, I'd never rule out going for it again, but it did feel a bit 'now or never'. In the run-up to Rio my training will be a bit different for the team pursuit; I'll be preparing for an intense effort of less than four minutes rather than keeping up a slightly lower intensity for 60 minutes.

What tackling the Hour did do, however, was put riding the 4,000m individual pursuit into perspective. After bashing out 54km, it's funny to think that in pursuit training those four kilometres can seem a bit long. That means it's likely that I will come back to London for the world track championships in March 2016 and try to win the individual pursuit 13 years after winning my first gold in Stuttgart. I might even combine it with another go at winning a madison title with Mark Cavendish. That would be a neat way to close both those books.

I was asked afterwards if the Hour was the hardest thing I'd ever done. My answer was, try leading the Tour de France for two weeks, looking over your shoulder all the time. This was 'only' one hour. Nothing can ever surpass the Tour in terms of intensity and difficulty, and its daily demands over nearly four weeks. The Hour is quite simple compared to the Tour de France, any stage race, or even a time trial on the road, because there are fewer variables. For example, you very rarely puncture on the track, and you'd be unlucky to crash. You get up on the boards and knock out 16.4sec laps for an hour. There are no 'what ifs'. It's not like Paris–Roubaix, for example, where you spend so much time thinking, 'If I get through the Arenberg Forest all right . . .' or, 'If such and such doesn't knock me off . . .' or 'If I don't puncture here . . .' With the Tour, you have to get through the first eight days without crashing, and even then, when you've found your 'open road', anything can happen, even people chucking tintacks on the tarmac on a mountain descent like in the 2012 Tour. With the Hour, you get to 46 or 47 minutes to go and you think it will never end – for a while afterwards I got flashbacks, I couldn't believe it was over – and there is huge pressure because it's such a lonely experience, but the lack of variables relieves a lot of the stress. That's why I like it, and that's why people like Alex Dowsett and Chris Boardman like it – it taps into our British time-trialling pedigree. It's quantifiable. It's pure.

As I go slowly round the track for that warm-down lap, it's an incredible feeling. I've joined that club: the Tour winners who've broken the Hour. I can't help but be a bit nostalgic; it was about this point that the old finish straight at the Eastway Circuit used to be. It's phenomenal to think what this site has become – they've even managed to get rid of the dip and the little hill and the freezing cold wind that used to make Eastway a perishing place to race. The biggest event that used to happen here was the March Hare, a day of racing in March with a decent crowd to watch the pros, but nothing special; now it's events like this: a crowd of 6,000, sold out, live on TV with a million and more glued to their sets.

It's a full-circle moment for me. Here I am on the site of my old stomping ground, the manky old circuit with the battered cafe and changing rooms where I used to

It was really special for me to have someone of the stature of Miguel Indurain there to support. I even got him to sign one of his jerseys for me

ride around in the Thursday League in the summer pretending to be Laurent Jalabert or Miguel after watching the Tour de France all afternoon. Twenty years on I'm in the same place, having beaten the Hour and stood with Miguel who has come to watch me do it. For a historian of bike racing, the Hour is a phenomenal record, and as a rider you end up comparing yourself to the others on the list. I'm still a fan at heart, and I was inspired so much by Miguel and all the other legends, although I never dreamed that I could be like them. Miguel is a big bronzed man from Pamplona; when you are a skinny little kid from Kilburn, you never imagine that one day you'll do what they've done.

The feats of the riders I watched in my teens like Indurain, Johan Museeuw, Rominger and the late Franco Ballerini all had such an influence on me, such a profound effect. I wouldn't be here today and have that love for the sport without them. In my case, it's not just down to the physical attributes that I have but that love of the history of cycling, that knowledge of what you are about to achieve and what it means. Without all those people I wouldn't have done what I've done, because I wouldn't have been in love with the sport.

In some ways, 15 years on it's irrelevant what I've achieved because I still see myself as the same person, who is still as much in love with the sport as ever. I'm a geek with my obsession with cycling history – I don't mind admitting it. As I got older, for a few years I forgot about that stuff – you're 25, 26, and you think, 'You can't still be a fan of cycling, you're too cool for that.' But as time has gone on I've embraced it. That's why I'm doing it today: because of the influence Miguel and all the other greats going back through to Eddy Merckx and Jacques Anquetil had on me when I was a kid. That's why I'm here, riding painfully around a velodrome in front of 6,000 people, unable to hear for the din, with a numb backside, sore legs and a massive feeling of relief. This one is for them.

Acknowledgements

I'd like to thank Cath, Ben, Bella, Heiko, Shane, Ernie, Debs, Emma, Smeggers, Dunne, McQuaid, Joe, Robbie, Helen, Robert, Julian, Simon Fuller, Juan, Tolo, Pedro, Sally, Greg, Raibin, Chris Boardman, Carsten, Fausto, Luciano, Martin in Majorca, Terry Dolan, Dave Brailsford, Team Ski, Andy, Viv, Dirty Barry, Fish, Amanda, Bastos, Rogers, Ste and Tiff, Ruth, Neil, Luke, Angela and William Fotheringham.

I'd also like to thank all those who supported the event including Sky, Vitality, Rapha, Pinarello, Jaguar, Vittoria, Speedplay, Fizik, Giro, SiS, SRM, Strava, Muc-Off, British Cycling, EIS, Lee Valley VeloPark, Sweetspot, UCI, XIX Entertainment as well as Matt, Frances, Bethan, Phil, David, and everyone else at Yellow Jersey Press and Two Associates.